P9-BBN-796

J 796.33264 COWBOYS GIL
Gilbert, Sara.
The story of the Dallas
Cowboys

NFL TODAY

THE STORY OF THE

DALLAS COWBOYS

FOUNTAINDALE PUBLIC LIBRARY DISTRICT
300 West Briarcliff Road
Bolingbrook, IL 60440-2894
(630) 759-2102

NFL TODAY

THE STORY OF THE DALLAS COWBOYS

SARA GILBERT

CREATIVE EDUCATION

PUBLISHED BY CREATIVE EDUCATION
P.O. BOX 227, MANKATO, MINNESOTA 56002
CREATIVE EDUCATION IS AN IMPRINT OF THE CREATIVE COMPANY
WWW.THECREATIVECOMPANY.US

DESIGN AND PRODUCTION BY BLUE DESIGN
ART DIRECTION BY RITA MARSHALL
PRINTED IN THE UNITED STATES OF AMERICA

PHOTOGRAPHS BY AP IMAGES (FORT WORTH STAR-
TELEGRAM), CORBIS (BETTMANN, TOM FOX/DALLAS
MORNING NEWS, DANE HOFF, IRWIN THOMPSON/
DALLAS MORNING NEWS), GETTY IMAGES (JONATHAN
DANIEL, DIAMOND IMAGES, JAMES DRAKE/
SPORTS ILLUSTRATED, FOCUS ON SPORT, GEORGE
GOJKOVICH, BILL FRAKES/SPORTS ILLUSTRATED,
SCOTT HALLERAN, GRANT HALVERSON, WESLEY HITT,
PAUL JASIENSKI, RON JENKINS/FORT WORTH STAR-
TELEGRAM/MCT, ANDY LYONS, RICHARD MACKSON/
SPORTS ILLUSTRATED, RONALD MARTINEZ, JIM
MCISAAC, AL MESSERSCHMIDT, RONALD C. MODRA/
SPORTS IMAGERY, GEORGE ROSE, JAMES D. SMITH/
ICON SMI, TONY TOMSIC/NFL, GREG TROTT/NFL
PHOTOS, TIM UMPHREY)

COPYRIGHT © 2014 CREATIVE EDUCATION

INTERNATIONAL COPYRIGHT RESERVED IN ALL
COUNTRIES. NO PART OF THIS BOOK MAY BE
REPRODUCED IN ANY FORM WITHOUT WRITTEN
PERMISSION FROM THE PUBLISHER.

LIBRARY OF CONGRESS CATALOGING-IN-PUBLICATION DATA
GILBERT, SARA.
THE STORY OF THE DALLAS COWBOYS / SARA GILBERT.
P. CM. — (NFL TODAY)
INCLUDES INDEX.
SUMMARY: THE HISTORY OF THE NATIONAL FOOTBALL LEAGUE'S
DALLAS COWBOYS, SURVEYING THE FRANCHISE'S BIGGEST STARS
AND MOST MEMORABLE MOMENTS FROM ITS INAUGURAL SEASON
IN 1960 TO TODAY.
ISBN 978-1-60818-300-5
1. DALLAS COWBOYS (FOOTBALL TEAM)—HISTORY—JUVENILE
LITERATURE. I. TITLE.
GV956.D3G55 2012
796.332'64097642812—DC23   2012031206

FIRST EDITION
9 8 7 6 5 4 3 2 1

COVER: TIGHT END JASON WITTEN
PAGE 2: CORNERBACK BRANDON CARR
PAGES 4–5: 1972 DALLAS DEFENSIVE LINE
PAGE 6: QUARTERBACK DON MEREDITH AND COACH TOM LANDRY

TABLE OF CONTENTS

DALLAS IS HOME TO PROFESSIONAL TEAMS IN ALL FOUR MAJOR SPORTS

Cowboy Country

Dallas, Texas, was originally intended to be a trading post. But by the time founder John Neely Bryan arrived at the fork of the Trinity River to build the post in 1841, most of his customers—the local American Indians—had been forced out of the area. So Bryan decided to establish a town instead. That town was so small that he was the settlement's postmaster, storekeeper, and judge; the first courthouse operated out of his home. Today, Dallas has grown into one of the 10 largest cities in the United States. It has one of the busiest airports in the world and is home to some of the biggest companies in the country.

Dallas is also home to some of the biggest football fans in Texas—and perhaps the U.S. Most Texans love football, whether it's played at the high school, college, or professional level. Friday nights are reserved for high school football games, and Saturday afternoons are spent cheering for one of the many local collegiate teams. But since 1960, residents of the "Lone Star State" have rooted most passionately on

LINEBACKER LEE ROY JORDAN REPRESENTED THE COWBOYS FROM 1963 TO 1976

✕Tex Schramm

PRESIDENT, GENERAL MANAGER / COWBOYS SEASONS: 1959—89

Tex Schramm was the first architect of the Cowboys. But many of Schramm's innovations extended far beyond Dallas. Some ideas, such as having dancing cheerleaders, were simply popular. Other ideas became such league-changing concepts that Schramm has been credited with almost single-handedly altering major aspects of the game. For example, while setting hash marks in the center of the field and giving the referee a microphone are actions taken for granted these days, they were major advancements when Schramm suggested them in the 1970s. Creating instant replay, implementing sudden-death overtime, and expanding the Wild Card playoff system are just some of the other innovations Schramm developed for the ever-evolving league. One of Schramm's main areas of focus, however, was player safety. Between 1974 and 1979, he lobbied to move the goalposts from the goal line to the end line, to ban helmet-slapping by defensive linemen, and to create the "in-the-grasp" rule to protect quarterbacks from injury. Schramm's reputation was so exemplary that he was named president of the World League of American Football when the NFL first tried to make itself an international sport in 1989.

SPEEDY WIDEOUT BOB HAYES BECAME ONE OF DALLAS'S FIRST OFFENSIVE STARS

Sundays, when they cheer for the team with the lone star on its helmet—the Dallas Cowboys.

The Cowboys were born of a rivalry between two leagues. In 1959, after repeatedly being denied a new franchise by the National Football League (NFL), Dallas millionaire Lamar Hunt retaliated by starting the American Football League (AFL) with seven other owners. Hunt's flagship team was called the Dallas Texans.

To compete with the newly formed rival, the NFL awarded an expansion team to another Dallas millionaire, Clint Murchison Jr. In 1959, before the team had been formally admitted to the NFL, Murchison hired Tex Schramm to be his general manager. Schramm, who had previously held the same position with the Los Angeles Rams, set up his first office in a corner of the Texas Auto Club. "People would crowd in there to map routes for trips, and I'd be over in a corner discussing player contracts on the phone," Schramm remembered. "Sometimes they'd listen in. The noise was unbelievable."

Murchison couldn't name a head coach before being awarded official franchise status, but he and Schramm knew who they wanted: New York Giants assistant and Texas native Tom Landry. They sidestepped the rule by signing Landry to a "personal services" contract. "People were calling him a young genius for what he had done with the Giants' defense," Schramm later said. "He was the only person I actually ever talked to about the job."

Schramm also had to get creative to assemble players for the unofficial team, including his top choice for quarterback, a two-time All-American named "Dandy" Don Meredith from local Southern Methodist University. Using cloak-and-dagger tactics, Schramm asked his old friend George Halas, owner of the Chicago Bears, for help in making the deal. Halas drafted Meredith and promptly traded him to Dallas. Schramm used a similar tactic to sign running back Don Perkins.

chramm's job became much easier on January 28, 1960, when the Dallas Cowboys were officially admitted into the NFL. Most of the early players, many of whom were drawn from a "player pool" of other teams' leftovers, were unremarkable—including veteran quarterback Eddie LeBaron, who was brought in to start while Meredith adjusted to the pro game. The Cowboys finished their first season with a 0–11–1 record. They won four games the next year and five games in 1962.

Even as their crosstown rivals, the Texans, won the AFL championship over the two-time defending champion Houston Oilers in 1962, the Cowboys believed they were on the right track. The fans did, too. The fierce competition for fans finally forced Hunt to move the Texans to Kansas City in 1963, where they became the Chiefs.

Dallas now belonged exclusively to the Cowboys—and the Cowboys offense now belonged to Meredith. He and Perkins led the offensive charge, while tackle Bob Lilly led the defense. Dallas had selected the fast and powerful pass rusher with its first-ever draft choice in 1961, then built the team around him by drafting defensive talent such as linebacker Lee Roy Jordan in 1963. Dallas brought ballhawking safety Mel Renfro and wide receiver "Bullet" Bob Hayes, a world-class sprinter, to the team in 1964.

In 1966, Dallas went 10–3–1 and made the playoffs for the first time. Over the next four seasons, the Cowboys would post a combined 42–13–1 record. In 1966, the young team charged all the way to the NFL Championship Game, where it was stopped by the mighty Green Bay Packers.

The First Texans

Texas's first professional football franchise, the Dallas Texans, was unable to last a full season in 1952. The team began with high hopes, as owner Giles Miller figured that Texas—a huge state with a long-standing reputation for great high school and college football—would be a perfect fit for a pro football franchise. "There is room enough in Texas for all kinds of football," Miller declared. But the 1952 Texans barely got off the ground and never approached a win. No wins also meant no fans. Miller lost so much money so quickly that he was unable to meet payroll. So, rather than stick it out and hope for a turnaround, he cut his losses early and returned his team to the league with five games left in the season. The league transferred the Texans to Hershey, Pennsylvania, and made them a road team. The gimmick worked, as the Texans finally got a win on Thanksgiving Day against the Chicago Bears. It would be an additional eight years before residents of the Lone Star State could cheer for another hometown professional football team.

THE 1952 TEXANS DID GRIDIRON BATTLE IN FRONT OF SOME VERY SMALL CROWDS

DON MEREDITH (#17) STRUGGLED IN THE "ICE BOWL," PASSING FOR 59 YARDS

In 1967, the Cowboys returned to wintry Wisconsin for another championship game against the Packers. The official game-time temperature was -13 degrees, with a windchill around -48—frigid conditions that led to the game's being called the "Ice Bowl." The cold overwhelmed Lambeau Field's turf heating system, and the field became a rock-hard sheet of ice. It also overwhelmed some players. Hayes, for example, inadvertently tipped off plays to the Packers. When he wasn't the intended receiver on a play, he put his cold hands in his pants to keep them warm. When Hayes was the intended target, he lined up normally with his hands out. The Packers keyed in on this and shut down the Cowboys' passing offense, handing Dallas a bitter 21–17 defeat. "I was just happy to get out of that game alive," Lilly said. "I'll never forget that game."

15

Bob Lilly

DEFENSIVE TACKLE / COWBOYS SEASONS: 1961–74 / HEIGHT: 6-FOOT-5 / WEIGHT: 260 POUNDS

It's no wonder Bob Lilly was nicknamed "Mr. Cowboy." Nearly everything he did was a Cowboys first—first draft pick, first multitime All-Pro selection, first inductee to the team's Ring of Honor, and first to represent Dallas in the Pro Football Hall of Fame. The Cowboys don't retire jersey numbers, but no player has ever worn number 74 in Dallas since Lilly retired in 1974. Armed with a rare combination of durability and skill, Lilly had exceptional field vision, catlike reflexes, and enough strength to fight through constant double- and triple-teams. And he never missed a regular-season game in his 14-year career. "I didn't think a man that big could be so quick," Miami Dolphins guard Bob Kuechenberg once said. A change of position in 1971 would alter the course of Lilly's career—and the Cowboys' fortunes—for the better. When coach Tom Landry moved Lilly from his normal defensive end position to the interior as a tackle, the famed "Doomsday Defense" suddenly gained its engine. And the Cowboys went from Super Bowl losers to champions in one year.

America's Team

Success breeds popularity. And in the 1970s, the Cowboys became so successful that their popularity spread far beyond Texas. Bob Ryan, now the vice president and editor-in-chief of NFL Films, came up with the title "America's Team" when he was preparing the Cowboys' 1978 highlight reel. "The Cowboys had just lost a crushing Super Bowl to the Steelers," Ryan explained. "I wanted to come up with a different twist on their team highlight film. I noticed then, and had noticed earlier, that wherever the Cowboys played, you saw people in the stands with Cowboys jerseys and hats and pennants." There's also the "Cowboys Factor" in television programming. "When in doubt, give them [the viewers] the Cowboys," football historian Beano Cook once said. And indeed, since 1966, the Cowboys have been viewed by millions in their annual Thanksgiving Day game. "[It] has helped give us our notoriety," Cowboys safety Bill Bates said. "Everybody is sitting around eating their turkey and watching the team with the star on the helmet. It's a national tradition." A 2011 Harris poll of football fans confirmed what millions already knew—the Cowboys are America's favorite football team.

TEXAS STADIUM, THE TEAM'S OLD HOME, COULD HOLD ABOUT 66,000 FANS

luxury liner *Titanic* smugly declared their state-of-the-art ship "unsinkable," seeing no need to provide lifeboat capacity for everyone onboard. On the night of April 14, 1912, more than 1,500 passengers and crew paid for this hubris with their lives after the ship collided with an iceberg and sank. But human catastrophes aren't always the unforeseen consequences of carelessness or folly. In the 1940s the leaders of Nazi Germany purposefully and systematically set out to exterminate all Jews, along with Gypsies, homosexuals, the mentally ill, and other so-called undesirables. More recently terrorists have targeted random members of society, blowing up airplanes and buildings in an effort to advance their political agendas.

The books in the GREAT DISASTERS: REFORMS AND RAMIFICATIONS series examine these and other famous disasters, natural and human made. They explain the causes of the disasters, describe in detail how events unfolded, and paint vivid portraits of the people caught up in dangerous circumstances. But these books are more than just accounts of what happened to whom and why. For they place the disasters in historical perspective, showing how people's attitudes and actions changed and detailing the steps society took in the wake of each calamity. And in the end, the most important lesson we can learn from any disaster—as well as the most fitting tribute to those who suffered and died—is how to avoid a repeat in the future.

"A Risky Business"

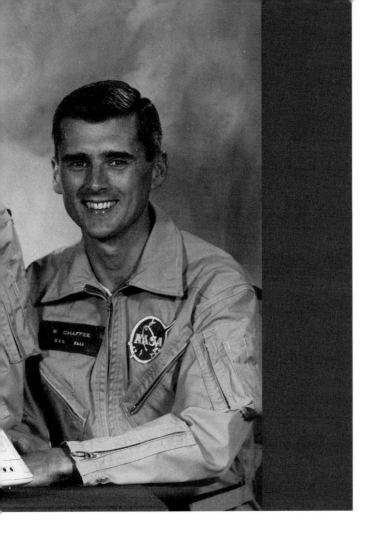

The three-man crew consisting of astronauts (from left to right) Edward H. White II, Virgil "Gus" Grissom, and Roger B. Chaffee was scheduled to fly the first flight of Project Apollo on February 21, 1967.

January 27, 1967
Kennedy Space Center

It had been a long day for the crew and support technicians at the National Aeronautics and Space Administration (NASA) launch center in Cape Canaveral, Florida. They had been running a "plugs-out" test on the Apollo mission known as A.S.-204. The test was a launch simulation, but it was taking place in the spacecraft on the launch pad, not in a flight simulator. Three astronauts sat in a capsule hundreds of feet in the air, perched atop the massive Saturn I-B rocket on launch pad 34. The plugs-out test would ensure that all the spacecraft's systems worked properly and give both the flight crew and the ground support technicians a

The charred exterior of Apollo Spacecraft 012, where the astronauts Grissom, White, and Chaffee lost their lives in a fire during a count-down simulation on January 27, 1967. The deaths of the Apollo crew shocked the nation.

chance to practice and work out any bugs. The commander of the mission, Virgil "Gus" Grissom, and his crew, astronauts Edward H. White II and Roger B. Chaffee, had been strapped in to the module for hours.

At about 6:20 P.M., the test was stopped yet again. As they waited, the astronauts and technicians looked over their data. The last part of the test for the day would be an emergency exit test— to check how quickly the astronauts could escape the command module should there be an emergency. But because of problems found earlier in the day, they wouldn't get to that test for some time.

Suddenly technicians heard a voice over the communications system: "Fire. I smell fire." Moments later Roger Chaffee's voice came through the headset sounding remarkably calm: "We've got a fire in the cockpit." A technician in the control room looked up at the array of television monitors in front of him, and focused on the screen showing the cone-shaped command module. There was a bright orange glow in the cabin porthole. A tense second or two passed as the men in the control room stared anxiously at their data monitors, waiting to hear the pad technicians say they had opened the module hatch and let the astronauts out.

The pad technicians rushed toward the module with fire extinguishers. Before they could get there, Chaffee's voice grew more agitated as the control room listened in horror: "We've got a bad fire. Let's get out. Open her up. We're burning up!" A short scream was heard a few seconds later. Then, just as the fire extinguishers were arriving—about 18 seconds since the first call of "fire"— an explosion blew out the outer panel of the command module, forcing the rescuers back.

Through the suffocating smoke and searing heat, the technicians fought to get to the module, rushing away from the flames when they could not breathe and then back again until finally, they succeeded in opening the hatch. But it was too late. No one could have survived the almost six minutes of inferno that had passed since Chaffee first reported the fire in the cockpit.

NASA consultant Don Babbitt, an employee of aerospace company North American Aviation, which had built the command module, was one of the first to look inside the charred cabin. Babbitt spoke into his headset a moment later: "I cannot describe what I saw."

Although officially known as flight A.S.-204, Grissom, White, and Chaffee's mission became known as *Apollo 1* at the request of their widows, even though the mission had never left the ground. It was an inauspicious start for a program that many hoped would be the greatest scientific and technological achievement in history—the landing of a man on the moon.

Gus Grissom had once publicly acknowledged the danger involved in the space program. Just one month before the disaster, he had remarked, "There's always a possibility that you can have a catastrophic failure." Expressing the mind-set of many test pilots like himself, Grissom had added, "Of course, this can happen on any flight. It can happen on the last one as well as the first one. So, you just plan as best you can to take care of all these eventualities, and you get a well-trained crew and you go fly."

"If we die, we want people to accept it," Grissom went on. "We are in a risky business, and we hope that if anything happens to us it will not delay the program. The conquest of space is worth the risk of life." Grissom was probably referring to accidents in space, however, and not on the launch pad.

Grissom's remark about being in a "risky business" was more than prophetic. By 1967, the new American space program had already operated 16 manned missions. Project Apollo would eventually involve 11 manned missions, in addition to untold numbers of unmanned rocket launches and other tests. During each launch, during each hour of each mission, several million things could go wrong, and almost any one of them could jeopardize the lives of the crew. The astronauts were riding a great ball of fire into the sky, and were trying to live and work in a place where there was no air, no water, no gravity, and no life.

What is remarkable, many NASA veterans have commented, is not that astronauts have died in the space program, but that so few tragedies have occurred. Although astronauts had been killed in plane crashes and other mishaps since the establishment of NASA in 1958, until the *Apollo 1* fire, none had died in the line of duty. In 1961 astronaut John Glenn acknowledged the danger of space travel. "We are going to have failures," he warned. "There are going to be sacrifices made in the program; we have been lucky so far."

How did NASA cope and keep the Apollo program going after the disaster? What changed after the *Apollo 1* fire? Was there any way to make this "risky business" safe?

Star Voyagers

Shown here during flight training are the Original Seven astronauts picked for Project Mercury: (from left to right) M. Scott Carpenter, L. Gordon Cooper Jr., John Glenn Jr., Virgil "Gus" Grissom, Walter M. Schirra Jr., Alan B. Shepard Jr., and Donald "Deke" Slayton.

Tensions between the United States and the Soviet Union peaked in the 1950s and 1960s, in what was known as the cold war. Each powerful nation feared the other's technological developments, particularly in missiles and rocketry, and competition between the two countries was intense. When the Soviets launched the first satellite, a small basketball-sized globe called *Sputnik I,* on October 4, 1957, the reaction of the American people and Congress was immediate panic. One month later the Soviets launched a second satellite, *Sputnik II,* which was six times heavier than the first satellite and carried the first space traveler—a dog named Laika.

Surpassing the Soviets in the space race took on paramount importance. Americans were shocked that the Russians had beaten the greatest country

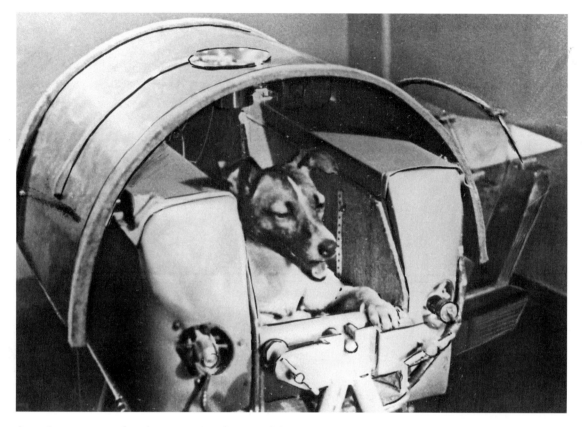

Americans were taken by surprise when the Soviet Union successfully launched *Sputnik I,* the first artificial earth satellite, on October 4, 1957. The idea of a Soviet satellite orbiting over U.S. soil terrified the nation, helping to initiate a "space race" between the two countries. The Soviets seemed to be winning the competition, when one month later, they launched *Sputnik II,* which carried a passenger, the dog Laika.

in the world in a technological arena. To make matters worse, as Americans saw it, their own space satellite program, Project Vanguard, was unsuccessful. Two months after *Sputnik I*'s successful launch, the *Vanguard 1A* rocket lost thrust and exploded two seconds after launch. The failure, coupled with the Soviet's success, painted a bleak picture for the future of the U.S. space program.

President Dwight D. Eisenhower was unwilling to put the American space program in the hands of the armed forces. The president believed that the exploration of space should be under civilian control. In July 1958, Congress passed and Eisenhower signed the National Aeronautics and Space Act. This legislation authorized the formation of a new civilian agency to lead the country's space program, the National Aeronautics and Space

Administration, which would be directly responsible to the president. It would use the personnel and research facilities of the National Advisory Committee for Aeronautics (NACA), a military agency formed in 1915 to carry out research in aerodynamics and air technology.

NASA officially began operations three months later, absorbing NACA's three major research laboratories: Langley Aeronautical Laboratory, in Hampton, Virginia; Ames Aeronautical Laboratory, near Palo Alto, California; and Lewis Flight Propulsion Laboratory, in Cleveland, Ohio. The three centers would later be referred to respectively as Langley, Ames, and Lewis Research Centers. The resulting workforce numbered 8,000 people. A year later, NASA took over a division of the Army Ballistic Missile Agency, directed by German rocket pioneer Wernher von Braun. It became the Marshall Space Flight Center, at Huntsville, Alabama—and the number of NASA employees grew by 5,000.

In the late 1950s it was well known, or at least suspected, that the Soviet Union was preparing to send a man into space—beyond the upper reaches of the earth's atmosphere. NASA's first manned space program, Project Mercury, would do the same. By October 1959 NASA as a whole had 13,000 employees, including the nation's first astronauts.

Few could pass the rigorous tests required of a NASA astronaut. The agency expected space flight would be highly stressful on the human body, so the astronaut candidates had to be male and younger than 40 years old. To fit into the Mercury capsule, whose weight and size were limited by the rocket power of the time, applicants had to be shorter than five feet eleven inches. NASA also required that astronaut candidates hold a bachelor's degree.

A further restriction was imposed on the applicant

pool when President Eisenhower declared the first astronauts would be military test pilots. In addition to the other requirements, then, the applicants had to be certified jet pilots who graduated from a test pilot school and had 1,500 hours of flight time (about 10 years of experience).

NASA screened the U.S. armed forces and found 110 men who fit the criteria. The agency invited all of them to interview. Because the job was so dangerous, NASA officials believed that few of the applicants would want to participate in the program. However, to their surprise, in the first group of 35 interviewees, 24 volunteered. Even more volunteered from the second group, so NASA canceled the rest of the invitations.

To narrow the pool NASA subjected the astronaut candidates to a variety of tests, including written tests, psychiatric examinations, technical tests, and medical reviews. By March 1959, 32 candidates remained. These men were invited to Albuquerque, New Mexico, to undergo medical testing. The tests, as described by author Michael Cassutt, were remarkable, and even a little weird:

> [The finalists] were subjected to seventeen different eye examinations; they had their brain waves measured; they were dunked in water to determine their bodies' specific gravity; they pedaled stationary bicycles against increasing loads; they had water dripped in their ears to study reactions to motion sickness; they were shocked, spun, prodded and punctured; their hearts and lungs were measured; and they were placed in chambers exposing them to extreme heat and cold.

Even these tests only reduced the 32-man candidate pool to 31. The men were subjected to psychological examinations at Wright-Patterson Air Force Base in Ohio, and then another round of tests in New Mexico.

In the end, the judges could not narrow the number of finalists down to six, and chose seven. The "Original Seven" astronauts were considered America's best and brightest pilots. The hopes of the nation rested on air force captains Donald "Deke" Slayton, Virgil "Gus" Grissom, and L. Gordon Cooper Jr.; marine lieutenant colonel John Glenn Jr.; navy lieutenant M. Scott Carpenter; and navy lieutenant commanders Walter M. Schirra Jr. and Alan B. Shepard Jr.

On April 12, 1961, Soviet cosmonaut Yury Gagarin became the first man to orbit the earth in *Vostok 1*. Three weeks later, on May 5, U.S. astronaut Alan B. Shepard Jr. flew the first mission of Project Mercury, a suborbital flight that made him the first American in space. And on

President John F. Kennedy shakes the hand of Alan B. Shepard Jr. while awarding him the NASA Distinguished Service Award in recognition of his suborbital flight into space on May 5, 1961. To Shepard's left are his wife and mother, while behind him stand the six other Mercury astronauts.

May 25, President John F. Kennedy declared that the U.S. government and its people should commit themselves "to achieving the goal, before this decade is out, of landing a man on the moon and returning him safely to earth."

This high-profile challenge, issued by a popular president, with a clear goal, a clear deadline, and a clear competitor meant that NASA would get the funding and the workers needed to succeed. NASA grew exponentially in a very short time. The space agency would eventually add Goddard Space Flight Center in Beltsville, Maryland, the John F. Kennedy Space Center in Florida, and the Manned Spacecraft Center (later renamed the Johnson Space Center) in Houston, Texas. By 1965, almost half a million people worked for NASA as employees or as contractors with research labs, universities, or private aerospace companies. The space agency had a budget of $1.8 billion.

Beginning with the Original Seven chosen for the Mercury program in 1959, astronauts experienced a fame almost unprecedented in American history. Astronauts were more than celebrities; they were heroes. They were the most visible men in the ever-growing space program. They were seen as the bravest, smartest, and healthiest men America could find. They would show the world not just that men could walk on the moon, but that American men would do it first.

The goal for Project Mercury was to put a man in space and achieve orbital space flight. The Mercury program would show that men could survive in space and perform work while there. The Gemini program would build on the strength of Mercury and use spacecraft built for two astronauts. The program's objectives, said NASA in 1961, were to put men into space for progressively longer periods of time, rendezvous and dock two vehicles in space, have astronauts perform "space walks" outside the vehicles, and develop reliable reentry procedures and pinpoint landing sites.

In 1962 NASA announced it would review applicants for a second group of astronauts. This time, the agency accepted applications from civilians, but only those who were experienced jet test pilots. Members of this group had to be U.S. citizens, have bachelor's degrees, and be younger than 35 years old. Because of the slightly larger capsule being used for the two-man Gemini missions, the height limit was raised to six feet.

Much more was known about space flight in 1962 than in 1959, and NASA eliminated some of the previous tests, considering them unnecessary. Two of the nine new astronauts selected by NASA were civilians—Neil Armstrong and Elliott See. Their colleagues in the group were Frank Borman, Charles "Pete" Conrad, Jim Lovell, James McDivitt, Tom Stafford, Edward H. White II, and John Young.

Even with the "New Nine," as the second group of astronauts was called, NASA realized that still more were needed. Requirements for the third group of candidates no longer included test piloting experience. Candidates needed to have bachelor's degrees in engineering or science, be U.S. citizens under 35 years old, and be pilots with 1,000 hours of flight time. In July 1963, NASA selected 14 new astronauts. This group included Edwin "Buzz" Aldrin, Charlie Bassett, Al Bean, Roger B. Chaffee, Michael Collins, Walter Cunningham, Don Eisele, Ted Freeman, Dick Gordon, Dave Scott, Russell Schweickart, and C. C. Williams.

In November 1963, the United States grieved at the sudden death of its president, John F. Kennedy, who was assassinated in Dallas, Texas. His successor, President Lyndon Johnson, continued to support many of Kennedy's programs, including NASA and space exploration. The agency's funding peaked from 1964 to 1966, during Johnson's term. In the mid-1960s, with the moon the single goal of the tens of thousands of NASA employees and contractors, anything seemed possible.

During this time the Gemini program essentially developed and trained astronauts, ground controllers, and spacecraft designers and builders, preparing them for Project Apollo. In early 1965 astronauts Gus Grissom and John Young flew on the first manned Gemini flight. A few months later, during the Gemini 4 mission, Ed White completed the first space walk. During the Gemini 5 mission, Gordon Cooper and Pete Conrad established a manned spaceflight duration record of eight days. NASA planned that Apollo would build on Gemini accomplishments, as engineers developed the technology needed to land a man on the moon.

NASA's next group of astronauts was selected with an eye toward this lunar exploration. The agency wanted scientists who could take full advantage of the opportunity the moon missions provided. For the first time, applicants were not required to be pilots; instead, each candidate would receive jet pilot training after selection. Interest in joining the ranks of the astronauts remained high, and 1,351 applications were received. NASA narrowed the number of candidates down to 400 (including four women) and finally to six. The names of this group were announced in June 1965: Owen Garriott, Edward Gibson, Joseph Kerwin, Curtis Michel, Harrison Schmitt, and Duane Graveline.

With so many missions in the works (Apollo was originally intended to include more than 40 flights), NASA decided that its current roster of 30 active astronauts was enough only for Project Gemini and the first few Apollo missions. In April 1966, the agency increased the numbers with the announcement of 19 more new astronauts and another 11 in August 1967.

From late 1963 to 1965, 10 unmanned rocket launches tested the reliability of Apollo escape and abort mechanisms, as well as the new Saturn booster rockets, which would carry the Apollo spacecraft into outer space. In 1966 three unmanned Apollo missions successfully tested the command service module, or CSM. (The spacecraft was referred to as the CSM when the command module, which carried the crew, was connected to the service module, which contained the rocket engine, life-support system, and fuel cells.) Finally, it was time to schedule a manned mission using the CSM in the first lunar program. Every astronaut at NASA was eager to be a member of the first Apollo crew.

"Get with It Out There"

Lying on their backs in molded, reclining seats, the three *Apollo I* astronauts endured hours of training in the command module simulator, following prelaunch checklists during practice countdowns.

3

To Virgil "Gus" Grissom, one of NASA's most experienced astronauts, fell the enviable position of commander of the first Apollo mission, whose purpose was to test the command module in earth's orbit. The booster rocket that would carry the capsule into space would be a Saturn I-B, a forerunner of the most powerful rocket ever built, the Saturn V.

A competitive and sometimes intimidating man, the 43-year-old Grissom was married and the father of two boys. Born in Mitchell, Indiana, he graduated from Purdue University with a degree in mechanical engineering in 1950, and joined the U.S. Air Force. He worked as a test pilot for several years, logging 4,600 pilot hours.

Grissom was one of the Original Seven selected by NASA in 1959. Two years later, in July 1961, he flew on the suborbital Mercury 4 mission, becoming the second American in space. At the end of the mission, upon splashdown, Grissom narrowly avoided drowning when his capsule, *Liberty Bell 7,* blew its hatch prematurely. In 1965 Grissom and John Young flew the first two-man mission, Gemini 3, in a spacecraft appropriately named *Molly Brown,* after "Unsinkable" Molly Brown, a survivor of the 1912 sinking of the *Titanic.* With the Apollo mission, Grissom would become the first man to travel into space three times, and the first to do so in three different spacecraft—Mercury, Gemini, and Apollo.

Assigned to Grissom's crew were Ed White and Roger Chaffee. Born in San Antonio, Texas, in 1930, White was the son of an air force general. He attended the U.S. Military Academy at West Point, New York, graduated in 1952, and earned a master of science degree in aeronautical engineering in 1959 from the University of Michigan. In between, Ed White earned his wings and flew F-86 and F-100 jet planes in Germany for four years. In 1959 he attended the Air Force Test Pilot School at Edwards Air Force Base in California. Eventually, he was assigned as a test pilot to Wright-Patterson Air Force Base in Ohio.

Ed White was selected by NASA in 1962 as one of the New Nine, the second group of astronauts. Also experienced with space travel, White had flown on the Gemini 4 mission in 1965, becoming the first American to "walk" in space. Like many American "space families," Ed White and his wife and two children lived in Houston, not far from the Grissoms.

Roger Chaffee was also a pilot, but unlike his fellow crew members he was new to space flight. The youngest of the three astronauts, Chaffee was born in Grand Rapids, Michigan, and he earned his bachelor of science

With just moments to spare, Gus Grissom is plucked from the ocean while his capsule, the *Liberty Bell 7*, sinks nearly three miles to the ocean floor below. The second American in space, Grissom attributed the loss of the Mercury 4 command module to a faulty explosive-powered hatch that blew open prematurely. Thirty-eight years would pass before the lost capsule would be located and, in July 1999, raised to the surface.

degree in aeronautical engineering at Purdue University in 1957. After graduation he became a navy pilot. In 1963 Chaffee began work on a master of science degree in engineering, but stopped later that year when he was selected by NASA in the third group of astronauts. He was also a husband and father of two.

Although a space rookie, Chaffee was confident in the new Apollo spacecraft. "I'd feel secure taking it up all by myself," he said during an interview in December 1966.

It was mainly because of the dangerous end of Grissom's Mercury 4 mission in 1961 that the Apollo capsule hatch was redesigned. Some engineers and even other astronauts had suspected that the *Liberty Bell 7* hatch had opened because of pilot error. But Grissom insisted that he did nothing wrong, that the hatch had blown by itself. His friend Sam Beddingfield, an investigator of the incident, found proof that the hatch could have blown by itself, and helped exonerate Grissom.

The hatch for the Gemini and Apollo missions was redesigned with the primary purpose of preventing accidental opening—and not necessarily ensuring quick access should there be an emergency. The new command and service module, referred to by its production number as Spacecraft 012, had a hatch secured by six bolts that under normal conditions took 90 seconds to open— inward. The crew member assigned to open the hatch, Ed White, sat on the center couch in the command module. He needed a special tool to unfasten the bolts and had to reach up behind his head to operate it. For exercise, White and his backup, Dave Scott, would practice opening the hatch, which was comparable to lifting 200 pounds at the gym.

For months, since being named commander of the mission called A.S.-204, Grissom and his crew had worked hard to ready the spacecraft. Yet changes had not

been incorporated as quickly as the astronauts had hoped. The computer programs had bugs to be worked out, the environmental control system (which regulated temperature, pressure, and atmosphere) malfunctioned, wiring shorted out, and communications systems broke down. Grissom had tried to work with the engineers, giving them the benefit of his experiences with the Mercury and Gemini programs, but to his annoyance, they didn't seem inclined to listen.

The astronauts would train in both the Apollo spacecraft and a mockup of the capsule, or flight simulator. The simulator was in even worse shape, from Grissom's perspective. With all the design changes being made, it

Two of the crew members of the first manned Apollo space flight, Gus Grissom (left) and Ed White (center) were experienced astronauts. Grissom had flown Mercury and Gemini missions, while Gemini astronaut White had become the first American to walk in space. Roger B. Chaffee (right) was the only novice crew member.

was difficult enough to ready the actual spacecraft, but the simulator was even further behind. Grissom had become so disgusted with the simulator that he hung a large lemon on its crew hatch, indicating his opinion of it; the practice capsule simply had too many problems. The mission commander was not merely a disgruntled employee—he was as devoted to the Apollo program as anyone, if not more so. Problems were to be expected in any new flight program, and Grissom did his best to get the mission off the ground on schedule.

On January 27, a "plugs-out" test, which is a practice countdown before launch and a major part of preparation for manned launches, was scheduled to take place in Spacecraft 012, although the rocket was not fueled. Any manned space mission, and particularly those of the Apollo program, required the immediate support of hundreds if not thousands of people. There was the astronaut crew, who for this test would be in the command module atop the giant Saturn I-B rocket on Pad 34. In the White Room, which connected the service tower to the spacecraft, a group of technicians were on standby to assist astronauts in case of emergency. Nearby was the Firing Room, which controlled spacecraft booster system checks. It was housed in a concrete blockhouse located a few hundred yards from the launch tower. Launch operations were monitored at the Automatic Checkout Equipment (ACE) Control Room, in the operations and control building, located about five miles away from the pad. Mission control, at the Manned Spacecraft Center in Houston, was also involved in the test, since it is responsible for controlling all manned space flights once the spacecraft clears the launch tower.

The morning of the test, the three astronauts had breakfast with Deke Slayton, the chief of the Astronaut Office, and Joe Shea, the head of the Apollo Spacecraft

Program Office in Houston. Slayton and Shea heard Grissom's complaints about the spacecraft. "If you don't believe it, you ought to get in there with us," Grissom said. Shea thought about it, and even rescheduled his flight back to Houston so that he could stay for the test. There would be just barely enough room for him in the module if he didn't wear a flight suit and lay on the floor almost under Grissom's seat.

At the last minute, though, the technicians informed Shea that it was impossible to rig up radio communications for him in time for the test. Grissom insisted, "It's really messy, we want you to go fix it." But Shea argued that his presence in the capsule would be pointless that

(continued on p. 36)

By the fall of 1966, construction of the new command module for Project Apollo was under way. Here, NASA astronauts Ed White (left) and Gus Grissom check out Spacecraft 012, being built by North American Aviation at its plant in Downey, California.

SOVIET SPACE DISASTERS

When the first human in space returned to earth, he bailed out of his spacecraft when it reentered the atmosphere and parachuted safely to the ground. His landing was witnessed by two peasants and a cow. One of the women, puzzled by his sudden appearance and orange suit, asked, "Have you come from outer space?" Yury Gagarin answered "Yes, would you believe it? I certainly have." When he saw the woman's startled expression, he added, "Don't be alarmed! I'm Soviet!"

The Soviet Union's space program achieved many firsts in the space race, but they did not come without disasters. In March 1961, just before Gagarin's flight, a cosmonaut named Valentin Bondarenko was killed by fire while training in an isolation chamber. But for more than two decades, until 1986, few people knew about this cosmonaut's untimely death. If American space engineers had heard this information, they would have known to avoid the pure-oxygen environment that was partly to blame for the deaths of the crew of *Apollo I*. However, the Soviet government was not eager to publicize its failures.

The first space-related mishap the Soviet people heard about involved *Soyuz I*. Launched on April 23, 1967, with 40-year-old Vladimir Komarov aboard, *Soyuz I* was probably intended to dock with another craft, *Soyuz 2*, to be launched a day later. But after launch, *Soyuz I* began functioning abnormally and the second launch—which Soviet officials denied was planned in the first place—was canceled. The Soviet capsule spun out of control for most of its 19 orbits. When *Soyuz I* finally did reenter earth's atmosphere, its parachutes opened at an altitude of 4.3 miles and the craft was still spinning. Komarov probably passed out during reentry. The twisted parachute ropes rendered the chutes useless, and the craft plunged to the earth at 500 miles per hour. (Soviet spacecraft always landed on the ground, as opposed to American craft, which were designed to splash down in the ocean.)

Although the burial of Komarov's ashes was televised, information about the mission was not released. An American technician at a listening post (a center for monitoring other countries' electronic transmissions) in Turkey, and amateur ham radio enthusiasts in Turin, Italy, reported many years later that Komarov's last communications had been frustrated responses to his flight controllers. "You've got to do something, I don't want to die," he said. "You are guiding me wrongly, you are guiding me wrongly, can't you understand?"

Disaster struck the Soviet space program again four years later. *Soyuz II* launched on June 6, 1971, with three cosmonauts: Georgi Dobrovolsky, Vladislav

The USSR launched the first human being to fly in outer space when 27-year-old Soviet cosmonaut Yury Gagarin orbited the earth aboard Vostok 1 *on April 12, 1961.*

Volkov, and Viktor Patsayev. The crew successfully docked with the USSR space station, called *Salyut*. Once aboard, the three cosmonauts activated the station's equipment, conducted several experiments, and made observations of earth. The 24 days they spent in orbit set a new endurance record. After a textbook reentry and landing, the three cosmonauts were found, still strapped in their seats, dead.

Soviet investigators found that sometime during the 20-minute reentry period, a spacecraft valve opened prematurely, leaking the cabin's oxygen into space. Depressurization took only seconds, and the cosmonauts, according to Soviet procedure, were not wearing pressure suits. They blacked out almost instantly, and resuscitation, by the time they landed, was impossible.

After his friend and colleague Komarov had died in 1967, cosmonaut Yury Gagarin had written this message to a friend: "The road to the stars is steep and dangerous. But we're not afraid. . . . Space flights can't be stopped." Less than a year later, in March 1968, Yury Gagarin became one more casualty of the space race when he crashed while test piloting a MiG-15 jet.

(continued from p. 33)

day: "You think I'm going to sit at your feet for four hours and not be able to communicate? You're nuts. . . . I'll come back Monday and do it in the simulator with you." Slayton, too, thought about joining the astronauts in the module, but decided everyone would be better off if he stayed in the Firing Room.

At about 1 P.M. the various groups were in position for the plugs-out test. The astronauts were suited up and in the command module, the pad technicians were on the launch tower, and the flight controllers and engineers were in their respective control rooms. Mission simulations at NASA were taken every bit as seriously as actual missions. Still, despite the importance of the plugs-out test, it was a routine operation, performed for each launch and not considered particularly difficult. The firefighting and medical teams were on standby, not full alert. Actual liftoff was scheduled for February 21, three weeks away.

As the test proceeded, Grissom grew increasingly frustrated. First, he noticed that the oxygen being pumped into his suit from the command module's supply had a sour odor. The test was halted, and the countdown resumed after about an hour. Finally, about 2:45 P.M., the astronauts were sealed into the module by the heavy, two-door hatch, covered with a third hatch on the boost protective cover (BPC), which remained unlatched. (The BPC lay over the command module during launch and was jettisoned before the craft reached orbit.) The cabin was pressurized with pure oxygen, to keep the capsule free of contaminants, and the test continued.

But then there were communications problems between the module, the Firing Room, and the ACE Control Room. Technicians made some modifications and eventually the astronauts could be heard in the Firing Room, but not the Control Room. And Grissom couldn't hear the Firing Room so well either. "How do you expect to get us to the moon if you people can't even hook us up with a ground station?" Grissom asked over his headset. "Get with it out there." Flight controllers debated whether to call off this test, and decided not to. They would correct the problem now—after all, the February 21 launch date was not so far away.

While the technicians worked on fixing the communications difficulty, the astronauts and others continued with other events in the mock countdown. By 6:20 P.M., they had gone as far as they could go and were just about at liftoff time, but the radio communications still were not working properly. The test was stopped at T minus 10 minutes (or 10 minutes before time of simulated liftoff). It was during this scheduled break in the test that Slayton, in the Firing Room, heard a brief, clipped transmission from the spacecraft. It sounded like "fire."

The charred interior of the *Apollo 1* spacecraft. Fire swept through the pure-oxygen environment of the command module, giving the three astronauts inside only seconds to try to unfasten and open an unwieldy six-bolt escape hatch.

"It Just Went *ZOOP!*"

The fact that the *Apollo 1* fire happened not in space, but on the launch pad seemed only to make the tragedy more appalling. But, as some astronauts remarked privately to each other, that it happened on the launch pad was a blessing in disguise. In space, there was no chance of finding out the causes and correcting whatever problems there were. Three more men, or even six, may have died because of the flaws in Spacecraft 012. "[I]f we had had the Apollo fire in orbit or going to the moon," one NASA engineer said, "we wouldn't have flown for another decade."

"I think we've got an excellent spacecraft," Roger Chaffee had declared in December 1966. "I've lived and slept in it. We know it. We know that spacecraft as well as we know our own homes. . . . Sure we've

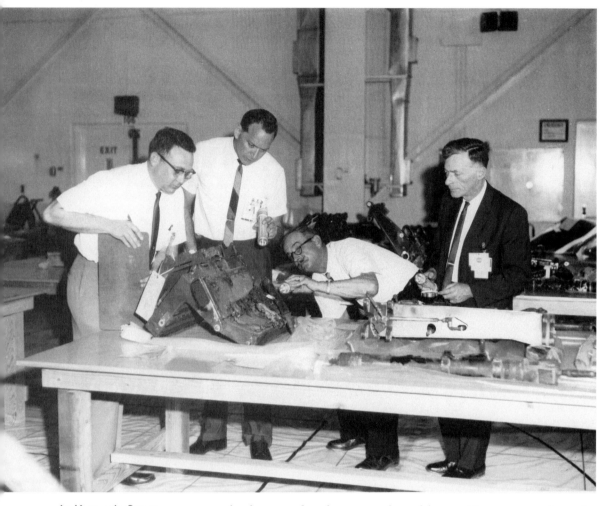

At Kennedy Space Center, members of the Apollo 204 Review Board Fire Panel examine a part taken from Spacecraft 012 as they work to determine the cause of the fire and other details of the disaster.

had some developmental problems. You expect them in the first one." But there were, apparently, more problems with the spacecraft than NASA or North American Aviation, the contractor that had built the command and service module, had admitted.

In the wake of the disaster, NASA imposed an information blackout until the organization could determine what went wrong. This lack of candor led some reporters to refer to NASA as "Never a Straight Answer." On February 3, NASA administrator James Webb set up an internal investigation board, known as the Apollo 204 Review Board, which was headed by Floyd Thompson, director of the Langley Research Center. The 21 investigative panels commenced work immediately. They would eventually hear the testimonies of a multitude of eyewitnesses and the professional opinions of some 1,500 experts.

Scott Simpkinson, a NASA engineer since the days of the Mercury program, was appointed to oversee the dismantling of the command module. The first task was to remove the astronauts' remains. The job was made difficult because the astronauts' space suits had melted in the 2,500°F heat, welding the men's bodies to the spacecraft interior. After this grisly job was completed, Simpkinson took a look inside the charred capsule.

Simpkinson later noted that an immense amount of support was given to the investigative panels. All the vast resources of NASA were available to any investigator, 24 hours a day. "If you wanted something made," he said, "it got made before you could blink an eye."

In the book *Apollo: The Race to the Moon,* authors Charles Murray and Catherine Cox explained how NASA provided the investigator with the tools he needed. For instance, Simpkinson wanted to get into the spacecraft to look around and take photographs without disturbing anything in the soot-strewn cabin: "Simpkinson wanted a Lucite floor? Cantilevered but strong enough to hold the weight of a few men at a time? Sculpted to fit the inside of the spacecraft? Hinged? The contraption was designed, fabricated, and assembled within the next two days."

Then Simpkinson's panel began what one engineer for North American Aviation described as "the most excruciating technical dissection of a machine I could ever imagine happening." The burned-out spacecraft was meticulously, painstakingly dismantled, screw by screw, bolt by bolt. Before a piece was moved or removed from the module, investigators took numerous photographs of it and filed several forms to receive permission to move it. Only after this procedure was followed would the piece be numbered, catalogued, and placed in a plastic bag.

Ten weeks later, the Apollo 204 Review Board submitted a 3,000-page report. Among the facts presented was the cause of death of the astronauts (attributed to asphyxiation resulting from carbon monoxide polluting their oxygen supply) and the approximate time of death (18 to 24 seconds after the fire was detected). The pure-oxygen environment, too, was blamed, for the volatile atmosphere caused the fire to quickly become an inferno. The exact sequence of events, the possible causes of the accident, and recommended procedures for improved safety and accident prevention were determined and set down.

Senate investigations dug up much more information about how NASA dealt with its contractors and about their methods of design, manufacture, and quality control. Questions were raised about how North American Aviation had acquired the NASA contract in the first place. It came to light that another bidder, the Martin Company, had been rated higher in overall technical ability. Some members of the press and of the U.S. Congress suspected that political ties had intruded on NASA's decision to use North American instead of Martin. But NASA insisted that North American Aviation had presented the most cost-efficient design. The agency noted that North American's proven expertise with building manned flight vehicles—including the experimental X-15 rocket plane, designed to travel at Mach 6 (six times the speed of sound)—had made that company a sound choice for building the command and service modules.

Even so, more than a year before the fire, Apollo program director Samuel Phillips had documented dissatisfaction with North American's progress on building the spacecraft. His notes from a visit to the company's plant in Downey, California, which came to be called the "Phillips Report," included the criticism that North American Aviation "was overmanned and that the . . . CSM programs could be done, and done better, by fewer total people, [who were] better organized." But the main problem was the large number of discrepancies between what NASA specified and what its contractor supplied. Phillips told North American, in effect, to clean up its act by April 1966, or the company would lose its contract. When that deadline came, Phillips and other NASA officials discovered, North American was indeed making progress—so work continued.

In the summer of 1966, NASA reviewed and accepted delivery of Spacecraft 012. But afterward, technicians and inspectors found several problems with the CSM, including defects in the construction of the life-support system and the cooling system. Correcting the problems slowed down the Apollo program and postponed the date of its first manned mission until the following year.

The Apollo 204 Review Board's report also identified the immediate cause of the fire. On the wall of the command module cabin, beside Grissom's seat, was a metal door leading to the Environmental Control Unit (ECU). Investigators surmised that the edge of this door had damaged a nearby cable. It was not designed to be in that spot, of course, but workers had left a bundle of wires running along the floor, with the cable resting temporarily on that bundle. The Teflon coating of the cable had been scraped, exposing a tiny section or two of wire underneath.

Something, perhaps a power surge, caused a spark in those exposed wires. Even in the pressurized pure-oxygen environment of the spacecraft, this spark would not necessarily have caused a fire. But near the scraped wire was an angled piece of tubing. Authors Murray and Cox explained its significance:

> This particular ninety-degree corner joint, one of hundreds in the tubing that interlaced the spacecraft, probably had sprung a leak. . . . Certainly even a small leak would help explain what happened, because the tubing carried a glycol cooling fluid which, when exposed to air, turned into fumes. The liquid was not flammable, but the fumes were.

Ten or more seconds after the electrical power surge, a spark could easily have found the leak and ignited the fumes. Nearby was Raschel, a flammable nylon netting, and Velcro, a favorite of the astronauts, used to fasten objects in place in the spacecraft.

NASA regulations stipulated that nothing that could cause a spark could be within four inches of anything that could ignite. It was already known that Velcro and Raschel netting were flammable—yet after the fire, investigators found that over 5,000 square inches of Velcro had been in the cabin, while only 500 square inches was allowed. Concerns about fire safety had been noted in a memo written by Apollo program head Joe Shea in August 1966: "The problem is sticky—we think we have enough margin to keep fire from starting—if one does, we do have problems. Suitable extinguishing agents are not yet developed." Wernher von Braun, director of the Marshall Space Flight Center, later remarked that "all surfaces of the spacecraft were supposed to be oxygen-compatible, and there shouldn't have been a fire."

But the preflight testing took place in a spacecraft

Investigators of the *Apollo 1* fire documented many examples of carelessness and sloppy workmanship found throughout Spacecraft 012, such as this metal wrench thoughtlessly dropped between two bundles of wire.

that was not yet ready to fly. Since August 1966 there had already been 623 changes made in the command and service modules—and more were being implemented daily. Technicians worked constantly on the spacecraft, and moved items around all the time. Some flammable foam-rubber pads were inside the cabin to protect wires and other mechanisms from being damaged by technicians. One of these pads had remained in the command module during the test, at Ed White's request. He didn't want to step on wires when it came time to open the hatch. There was no way to wait until everything was fixed and still keep the astronauts in training.

One of the designers of the Apollo spacecraft, Caldwell Johnson, formerly of Langley Research Center, made a disturbing discovery just after the fire. He ran into colleague Tom Markley's office at NASA carrying a

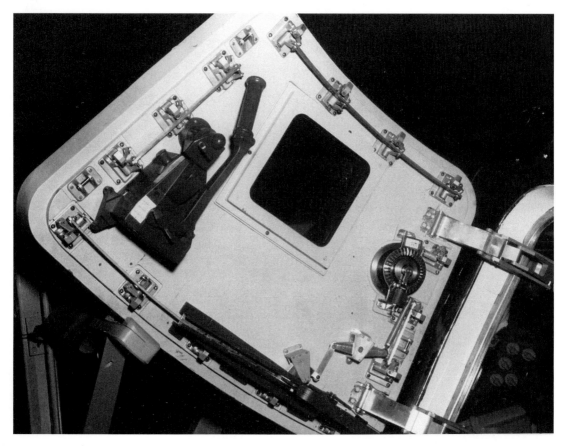

One of the many changes resulting from the *Apollo I* fire investigation: a new hatch for the Apollo command module designed to open within seven seconds. This August 1967 photo shows the hatch-opening mechanism, at left.

film of his findings and a movie projector. "Let me show you how this damn stuff explodes in pure oxygen," Johnson swore of the Velcro and netting. Markley was shocked: "It just went *ZOOP!* It was unbelievable. The stuff burned like you couldn't imagine."

The command module for a later mission, Spacecraft 017, had been shipped to Cape Canaveral from the North American Aviation plant in California and inspected about two weeks before the fire. As a result of the disaster in Spacecraft 012, NASA conducted another, more thorough inspection of the new CSM. Engineers found 1,407 problems, including sloppy workmanship, messy bundles of wiring, and even dozens of scraped wires.

Many changes in equipment, policy, and procedures

were made at NASA after the fire. The hatch, for one, was redesigned. Although it was not an explosive hatch, like the type used on some aircraft and on Grissom's ill-fated *Liberty Bell 7,* the new hatch nevertheless could be opened in seven seconds. New fire-resistant space suits were developed, nylon netting was replaced with more fire-resistant plastic materials, and simulators were severely fire-tested. NASA used the less dangerous oxygen/nitrogen mixture in all future ground tests, but did continue to use the pressurized, pure oxygen atmosphere during actual missions, partly because of the difficulty involved in overhauling the entire program to allow for a separate nitrogen system. But safety measures, particularly for ground tests, were improved. And the spacecraft's 12 miles of wiring were rerouted and better insulated. All these changes took time, and a manned Apollo spacecraft did not fly for 21 months following the fire.

Joe Shea, as head of the Apollo Spacecraft Program Office, felt personally responsible for the deaths of the astronauts. After the fire, he was transferred to another post and later resigned. His wife remarked that it was a full year before she heard him laugh. Joe had received a gift from Gus Grissom in August 1966, at the end of the review meeting during which Spacecraft 012 was officially approved. It was a photo of the three Apollo astronauts, posed as if praying over a small model of the capsule on a table before them. Grissom had announced to the room, "Joe advised us to practice our backup procedures religiously, so here we are practicing." Everyone laughed. The caption on the photo read, "It isn't that we don't trust you, Joe, but this time we've decided to go over your head." After the disaster, Shea kept the photo in a frame next to his front door, never entering or leaving his home without seeing it.

Gus Grissom's widow, Betty Grissom, accepts the condolences of President Lyndon B. Johnson, as he presents her with the American flag that covered her husband's coffin. Funeral services were held at Arlington National Cemetery, Virginia, on January 31, 1967.

The attitude of NASA and North American Aviation employees, particularly the technicians and engineers responsible for the command module, also changed drastically after the fire. "[O]nce the fire occurred, the flight schedule came to a screeching halt and everybody stopped and took stock," said one engineer. He noted how there was time now to work on "all of these things that everyone had in their back pocket that they should have worked on, and hadn't had a chance to." Clearly, the sheer number of people involved in the design, building, and operation of the command module—not to mention the other components of the launch vehicle—meant that everyone needed to be concerned that no problem would ever slip through the cracks again.

Gus Grissom and Roger Chaffee were buried with full honors at Arlington National Cemetery, in Virginia; Ed White was buried at the U.S. Military Academy in West Point. It took a long time for Apollo program participants to work through the tragedy, the guilt, and the blame. Project Apollo would eventually overcome the crisis in a triumphant manner. But for the three astronauts and the families they left behind, improvements made on the Apollo spacecraft came too late.

Once the United States
government achieved a
successful lunar landing,
it looked to set new goals
for the space program.
With the Space Trans-
portation System (STS),
or shuttle system, NASA
sought a more economical
approach to space travel
and exploration through
reusable spacecraft.

Uncharted Territory

The result of the newly galvanized force of workers at NASA and North American Aviation was that the Apollo command and service modules became one of the most successful designs of a spacecraft. Fifteen of them were built for the Apollo program, and each performed admirably. The first manned Apollo flight, *Apollo 7,* launched on October 11, 1968, and successfully rendezvoused with a Saturn booster rocket stage. Despite serious problems on later missions—*Apollo 12* was struck by lightning and still functioned; *Apollo 13* spent three days in space without electricity, and powered up again before reentry—by the end of the Apollo program, the astronauts had come to love their spacecraft.

Apollo 11 entered the history books when Neil Armstrong and Buzz Aldrin became the first humans to set foot on the moon. Five more

The Apollo lunar landing program proved a tremendous success. As this picture taken during the *Apollo 15* mission shows, not only did Americans leave their footprints on the moon but they also retrieved rock samples, conducted experiments, and even drove on the lunar surface in an electric cart (the Lunar Rover, on the right).

successful lunar missions followed, during which astronauts brought back moon rocks and performed dozens of scientific experiments. The Apollo program indeed established the dominance of the United States in the space race.

In December 1972, *Apollo 17* returned to earth from the last trip to the moon. Now that competition with the USSR was over and the goal of manned lunar exploration was met, NASA found itself justifying its continued existence. Increasing social unrest—particularly because of American involvement in the Vietnam War—had diverted public focus from, as well as funding for, the space program. Under the administration of President Richard

M. Nixon, NASA had to fight for its very survival.

It was certain the space program would continue in some form—very few people, if any, wanted a complete halt to American space exploration. But what would NASA *do*, exactly? Go to Mars? Build a space station like the Soviet Union's *Salyut*? Build a base camp on the moon? And how much would it cost?

In 1969, a Space Task Group chaired by Vice President Spiro Agnew had determined three possible long-range plans for NASA. The proposals involved building space stations, bases on the moon and Mars, and various shuttles to refuel and resupply the stations and bases. The least expensive of the three plans, at an estimated annual cost of $4 to $5.5 billion, proposed the development of a space shuttle and an earth-orbit space station. The most expensive plan, estimated to cost from $8 to $10 billion per year, called for manned missions to Mars, a lunar space station, a large earth-orbit station, and a shuttle. Besides making the argument that humans were born to explore, NASA argued that an extensive space program created jobs and stimulated the American economy. At the same time, NASA hoped to show that the space stations and shuttles could be economically affordable.

The Nixon administration believed that NASA should reduce the overall cost of space operations, which dashed the space agency's grand plans for journeys to Mars. However, the president did think an earth-orbit space station was a suitable long-term goal. The leadership of NASA, which included administrator Dr. James C. Fletcher and deputy administrator Dr. George Low, emphasized that the shuttle program, unlike Apollo, would not require any new technological innovations. With sufficient funding, the NASA officials promised, the space shuttle could fly by 1978. The possibility of economical space flight appealed greatly to the American people and their government representatives. In January 1972 President Nixon announced his support for a shuttle program; however, he did not approve a base or station for the shuttle to travel to.

NASA accepted shuttle design proposals from the aerospace companies Convair, Lockheed, and North American Rockwell (previously North American Aviation). Each plan included two huge crafts, one lifting the other almost to orbit, the second doing the rest of the work. Each proposed design cost $10 to $12 billion.

Because NASA's budget was shrinking in the 1970s, the space agency could not use any of the three proposals. A less expensive shuttle design consisting of three main components was eventually finalized: a disposable external fuel tank (or ET), two reusable solid rocket boosters (or SRBs), and a reusable orbiter. The reusable components would lower the overall costs, and although the disposable fuel tank component would increase operating costs, NASA could put off that budget expense until the 1980s. Meanwhile, the short-term costs were low, enabling NASA to obtain funding from reluctant politicians.

The shuttle's external tank is just that—a 154-foot tall fuel tank that carries almost one-half million gallons of liquid hydrogen and liquid oxygen propellants. The ET provides fuel for the orbiter's three main engines, which operate for about eight and a half minutes from liftoff until the shuttle reaches orbit. Then the disposable tank is jettisoned to burn up in the earth's atmosphere.

Attached to the opposite side of the ET are the two solid rocket boosters, each almost 150 feet tall. These boosters provide a brief, powerful thrust to push the orbiter into space. In fact, the SRBs provide 75 percent of the thrust in the first two minutes of flight. Afterward, they fall by parachute into the ocean, where they are retrieved and refurbished before being used on the

MR. D.D. MYERS   DR. J.C. FLETCHER   DR. G.M. LOW

next shuttle mission.

The 122-foot-long orbiter is, of course, the component that orbits the earth. The black and white, delta-winged craft carries a crew of six or seven and is designed to carry heavy payloads such as satellites or telescopes in its 60-foot-long cargo bay. At the end of the shuttle mission, the orbiter returns to earth by landing like an airplane on a runway at either Kennedy Space Center or Edwards Air Force Base in California. After landing in California, the orbiter is ferried back to Florida on top of a Boeing 747 jet.

Most people say "the space shuttle" when they really mean "the orbiter." But the term "space shuttle" applies to the system of all three components when assembled together on the launch pad, sometimes called the "stack."

During a March 1972 press conference, Dale D. Myers, associate administrator for the Office of Manned Space Flight; Dr. James C. Fletcher, NASA administrator; and Dr. George M. Low, NASA deputy administrator, lobby to convince the American public of the value and the need for funding a new space shuttle system.

NASA's official term for the shuttle is Space Transportation System, or STS. The shuttle system was designed to be used for approximately 200 flights.

The U.S. Air Force had agreed to help fund the shuttle program, since its own funding for a Manned Orbital Laboratory was cut in 1971. But this willingness actually made the job tougher for NASA, because the air force had its own ideas and requirements regarding the design, cargo bay size, and other aspects of the shuttle system. The V-shaped delta wings, for example, would increase the landing speed and angle of the orbiter—and the air force insisted on delta wings so that the orbiter had cross-range capability. In other words, the delta wings would enable the spacecraft to land on a runway far off to one side of its orbital track, but would require a much faster landing speed than a craft with a passenger airplane wing design. The air force also insisted on a vessel that could carry 40,000 pounds, whereas NASA had planned for only a 25,000-pound payload capacity.

However, other shuttle design requests were rejected. Turbofan engines, which would have enabled the orbiter to circle around and try again should the first landing approach be too difficult or unsafe, were eliminated because the engines would increase the weight of the spacecraft. Similarly scrapped because of weight considerations was an Abort Solid Rocket Motor, which would have allowed the orbiter to fly free of the boosters and land safely if anything went wrong during the first two minutes of a launch.

In the matter of designing emergency systems for the spacecraft, the shuttle differed from the Apollo craft in one important way: the level of safety was determined not by the scientists and engineers designing the craft but by the politicians setting the budget for shuttle development. For example, the less expensive solid-fuel rocket boosters would be used instead of the much safer liquid-fuel boosters. The fuel in the SRBs is a rubbery mixture of aluminum powder and ammonium perchlorate—more powerful than anything except liquid hydrogen and oxygen. Solid-fuel boosters are easier to reuse than liquid-fuel boosters, but cannot be shut off once ignited. Hence SRBs were a cheaper, but less safe, option. Even plans for an emergency exit system, which would shoot the orbiter crew cabin free of the launch stack in an emergency, were scrapped because of the cost.

One prelaunch safety feature of the shuttle system allows astronauts to quickly escape the orbiter by means of an emergency access arm, located on the launch tower. Steel baskets strung on thick cables await each crew member, who can jump into the basket, pull a rip cord, and glide down the slide-wire to a ground bunker located hundreds of feet below and away from the stack.

In case of an emergency occurring after the SRBs are jettisoned, the orbiter can set down at emergency landing sites at Kennedy Space Center or at runways in Africa or on the island of Crete. But from the time the SRBs ignite until they fall away two minutes later, there is no escape system. No other abort mechanisms were planned for the shuttle, making the machine a truly unusual system for a manned spacecraft.

Existing Apollo technology had to be redesigned for use in the new orbiter. On the Apollo command modules, the heat shield was not intended for reuse, so it simply burned up on reentry, when temperatures outside the craft reached nearly 3,000°F. But the orbiter was a reusable craft that would be exposed to temperatures as low as minus 250°F in space as well as the high temperatures of reentry. The final shuttle design called for the installation of hundreds of heat-resistant tiles installed on the outside of the orbiter. The weight of these tiles, coupled with the orbiter's heavy payload capacity, meant a design similar to the Apollo rocket could not be used for the new shuttle. A lighter, more powerful engine had to be developed.

The estimated cost of the final shuttle design came to $5.15 billion—just about the limit that Congress had imposed. Work on the new Space Transportation System began in August 1972. Construction of its various components was contracted out among a host of aerospace companies: the engines would be built by Rocketdyne; the orbiter, by North American Rockwell (later renamed Rockwell International); the solid rocket boosters by Thiokol; the external tank by Martin Marietta Corporation; the heat shield by Lockheed. In addition to this plethora of companies, Rockwell and Thiokol alone subcontracted work to 18,000 smaller companies.

Responsibilities for overseeing the design and construction of the space shuttle components fell to various NASA centers across the nation. Johnson Space Center in Houston oversaw work on the orbiter and the simulators; Marshall Space Flight Center in Huntsville reviewed work on the engines, boosters, and external tank; and Kennedy Space Center was in charge of shuttle assembly, launch, and servicing.

Three years later, the first shuttle engine tests were run. Like so many other components of the shuttle system, the engines were built "top-down" rather than "bottom-up." This means that instead of testing individual parts and then building the system, the contractor builds the complete system and then tests it. Because of the time constraint, it was not possible to test the engines' individual parts—instead inspectors tested entire engines while still developing certain components.

This process proved to be expensive. By 1977 four engines had been ruined during tests—a bad sign. In

1978 technicians discovered seven faults, and two more engines failed during testing. The "top down" process of testing doubled the cost of engine development.

Other problems surfaced as well. In September 1977, Thiokol performed a "hydroburst" test on its solid rocket boosters. The SRBs were made of segments held together at specially designed joints. Each joint was connected by two O-rings, which were designated as primary (essential for holding the joint in place) and secondary (considered a backup part). When the boosters were operating, the rubber O-rings would expand to make a seal, thus keeping the hot gases inside the booster. However during the September test, Thiokol discovered that the joints between the booster's sections

The final shuttle design consisted of three main components: a disposable external fuel tank (ET), two reusable solid rocket boosters (SRBs), and a reusable orbiter. The stack (as the three components together are called) would launch like a rocket from a pad in Florida, but the orbiter would land like an airplane on the other side of the country, in California.

did not perform well. Nevertheless, the company opted not to redesign the joint. On several occasions NASA engineers from the Marshall Space Flight Center disagreed with this decision. Nevertheless, the SRB design was approved on September 15, 1980.

From 1978 to 1979, there were massive delays in the schedule because of problems with the orbiter's heat-resistant tiles, as well as other components. NASA needed more money and the government and public were growing disgusted—the projected date of the first shuttle launch was repeatedly pushed back. The first launch was set for November 1979, then rescheduled again and again over the next two years.

"NASA had no need to feel ashamed of this," insists author Claus Jensen—the agency was, after all, in uncharted territory: "The problem was, however, that for ten years they had been telling Congress and the nation something quite different"—in effect, that NASA was not in uncharted territory, that the project would be almost easy for the same agency that had sent men to the moon. But engineers and technicians at NASA knew better—the space shuttle program depended on new knowledge and new technological expertise.

NASA's own style of management and organization had undergone serious changes during the 1970s. NASA administrator Dr. James Fletcher (1971–77) and his successor, Dr. Robert Frosch (1977–81), had successfully argued for funding for the shuttle system. But their arguments for economy led to a change in NASA itself. Now it seemed to many veterans of Apollo that the bosses didn't want to hear about problems—problems required more tests, which cost money. Problems, or even differences of opinion, indicated that NASA was wrong.

For a long time the space agency had prided itself on not being a typical bureaucracy, but a technological corporation with a famous "can-do" attitude. But during the late 1970s and early 1980s, senior management began to fear that any indication of problems or weakness would result in cuts in government funding.

From the beginning of the space program, NASA had maintained deliberately strict quality control over the workmanship and procedures provided by its private contractors. NASA was aware that the fire in *Apollo 1* had occurred because of discrepancies between the quality that NASA wanted and what its contractors supplied. This emphasis on quality control meant that before a contractor's products were used, they were subjected to detailed testing.

As NASA's budget shrank during the 1970s, private aerospace industries wooed experts away from NASA to work at their companies. These firms often had contracts with the space agency. So the highly educated and well-trained engineers and technicians who used to work *at* NASA now worked *with* NASA, as employees of Boeing, General Dynamics, and Lockheed. Early on in the space program, NASA would send its own personnel to inspect contractors' work. Now with a shortage of NASA engineers, inspections were more likely to be done by the contractors' own employees. At the same time, state and federal military funds that had previously gone to NASA were being funneled to leading educational institutions such as California Polytechnical Institute and Massachusetts Institute of Technology, which also attracted potential employees away from NASA.

By the 1980s, NASA's quality control system had eroded—and so had its own internal safety control system, which had been put in place after *Apollo 1*. NASA changed during the 1970s from the famous can-do club of the Apollo days, to an administrative bureaucracy.

Piloted by astronauts John
W. Young and Robert L.
Crippen, the shuttle
Columbia blasts off from
Kennedy Space Center
on April 12, 1981, at the
beginning of its first voyage
into space. The launch of
the new Space Transporta-
tion System marked the
beginning of an era of
reusable spacecraft.

The Flying Brickyard

6

In September 1976, Rockwell International Corporation rolled out the first space shuttle orbiter, named *Enterprise*. It was built as a test vehicle, so its engines and heat-resistant tiles were mock-ups, but it did have the orbiter's proper weight and instrumentation. Four months later, the new orbiter was transported to Edwards Air Force Base for approach and landing tests. From February through November 1977, astronauts Fred Haise (a veteran of *Apollo 13*), Gordon Fullerton (originally trained for the air force's Manned Orbital Laboratory), Joe Engle, and Dick Truly tested the *Enterprise*'s glide-landing capabilities. Ferried on the back of a Boeing 747, the test shuttle was then launched from an altitude of about 22,000 feet. These tests went well, although there was no way to really test the craft from orbit to landing.

Rockwell International Corporation in Palmdale, California, prepares to roll out Orbiter 101, later named *Enterprise,* after the spaceship on the popular television program *Star Trek.* Completed in September 1976, the orbiter was subjected to approach and landing tests the following year at the Dryden Flight Research Center, NASA's flight testing center in Edwards, California.

The flight of the first orbiter equipped for space flight, christened *Columbia,* would be the real test. *Columbia,* after all, would have to enter the earth's atmosphere at 400,000 feet, at a speed of Mach 22—that is, 22 times the speed of sound—and glide to a landing on the first try. Appropriately, shuttle pilots dubbed the spacecraft "the Flying Brickyard." Twice the weight of the Apollo craft, the 90-ton orbiter loses 3 feet in altitude for every 15 feet it "glides." It comes in for a landing at an angle of 22 degrees and a speed of 330 miles per hour. It must raise its nose to slow its speed to between 195 and 240 miles per hour, compared to a DC-9, which lands at 135 to 155 miles per hour, and which weighs considerably less.

Landing the orbiter is a particularly important part of training for astronaut pilots. The four onboard computers control everything in the orbiter by a "vote" system. If one computer disagrees, the flight can continue, but if two computers differ, the orbiter must land. During a flight, the crew must load the flight programs and the landing programs into the computers at the appropriate times. A fifth computer is an emergency backup system; it contains only the launch and landing programs. On the first orbiter flights, the pilot and commander would be responsible for lowering the landing gear at the right moment and applying the brakes—and both are more dangerous than they sound, allowing only a very small margin for pilot error. On later flights, brakes would also be controlled by computer.

The reason for such extensive computer control is not that the human pilots are not trustworthy. On the contrary, the shuttle is perhaps the most difficult craft in the world to operate and its pilots are trained accordingly. The reason, rather, is safety. Human reactions are far too slow to guide this particularly complicated machine to a landing. The four computers constantly receive detailed data from 2,000 sensors in all parts of the shuttle's systems. The computers use that data to calculate the shuttle's reactions to the rapidly changing conditions of its environment—at the rate of 50 "votes" per second. No one person, no matter how well-trained and intelligent, could possibly do the job the computers do in fractions of a second.

Even with all the delays in engineering design and development, getting the first shuttle up in the air was something of a rush job. In November 1980 the last heat-resistant tiles were applied to *Columbia;* in December the engines were tested and finally ran without exploding.

The first launch of NASA's Space Transportation System finally took place on April 12, 1981—exactly 20 years to the day that Yury Gagarin orbited Earth. The successful mission ended two days later, when astronauts

John Young and Robert Crippen made a perfect landing at Edwards Air Force Base in California. They emerged, after performing final checklists, to cheering crowds. Normally unemotional in public, Young punched the air and whooped with delight.

Columbia's first mission was officially a test flight. Although six test flights had been planned, the shuttle was declared operational after the fourth flight ended on July 4, 1982. Some engineers, as well as critics, worried that four test flights were not enough—there had been no accidents, but there still were serious problems.

On the first flight, heat-resistant tiles fell off the orbiter. The second flight, after a delayed launch, ended three days early because of a fuel cell failure. On the third, cameras and radio equipment, as well as the toilet system, failed. On the fourth, both boosters were lost when their parachutes failed to open, and the steering was adversely affected by steam rising from wet tiles. Other problems cropped up with the main engines, the computer systems, and the brake system.

The second test flight of *Columbia* also exhibited an unexpected problem with the SRB joints. After the mission, inspectors noted that the joints between the booster segments did not seal as well as intended. The reason was joint rotation: the intense heat and pressure inside the booster caused its walls to bow outward. The bowing caused the joints, which were stronger than the walls because they were three times as thick, to twist and stretch. Engineers were concerned that this joint rotation could keep the O-rings from doing their job.

Another problem on the second flight was "blow-by"—the hot gases inside the booster partially eroded the O-ring seals. This problem of O-ring erosion would be studied and addressed by Thiokol (renamed Morton Thoikol in 1982) and NASA engineers over the next

several years, with varying effects. It was, at the time, only one of hundreds of minor concerns about the shuttle—but in a few years, this problem would receive international attention.

During the fifth space shuttle mission, it was discovered that two essential plastic pins were missing from the $2 million Extra-Vehicular Activity (EVA) space suits. Because the suits were not airtight, a planned space walk had to be canceled, to the annoyance of the astronauts. However, when the mission returned, inspectors found that one of the suits also had metal filings in its exhaust vent. If the suit had been worn, it would have ballooned and exploded, killing the astronaut and possibly blowing out a wall of the orbiter in space.

Problems—even serious ones—were to be expected in

NASA crew commander John Young and pilot Robert L. Crippen pose with the model of space shuttle Orbiter 102, *Columbia,* the first orbiter to fly in space. One of their biggest challenges would be to safely land the 90-ton spacecraft, which would reenter the earth's atmosphere at 22 times the speed of sound.

Columbia rides piggyback on a Shuttle Carrier Aircraft (SCA), which transports the orbiter back to Florida after a California landing at Edwards Air Force Base. The 1,625-acre Johnson Space Center and the municipality of Nassau Bay, Texas, appear below.

the development and operation of such a complicated and brand-new system as the space shuttle. The STS was clearly a program still in development and not fully operational. The same had happened in NASA's glory days, during Project Mercury, but now there was a big difference: during Mercury NASA admitted when it had problems, which helped get them solved. But problems did not fit the image that NASA had painstakingly cultivated: the perception of the space shuttle providing routine, safe space flight. As author Claus Jensen noted, errors were no longer acceptable: "Now, every single breakdown was regarded as an embarrassing exception, to be explained away and then corrected, under wraps, as quickly as possible—so as not to damage the space shuttle's image as a standard piece of technological equipment." Inside the NASA organization, though, people knew better.

To justify the enormous expenditure for the Space Transportation System, NASA had planned an ambitious flight schedule; each launch would cost $10.5 million. By running 30 flights per year, NASA consultants figured, the space shuttle could pay for itself. NASA officials anticipated a schedule of one flight per week, or at least one every two weeks, and even predicted making a profit on 581 flights to take place between 1980 and 1991.

In 1983 NASA consulted several airline companies about scheduling—since they should know something about routine flight. Astronaut Frank Borman, a veteran of the Gemini 7 and Apollo 8 missions, was shocked to hear about such plans: "I called them and told them they were crazy. The shuttle is an experimental vehicle, and will remain an experimental, highly sophisticated vehicle on the edge of technology." Other NASA personnel, like Bill Lilly, had commented in the 1970s, when the shuttle was still being designed, that it would remain an experimental craft into the year 2000.

Despite the difficulties of the first shuttle flights, NASA continued to launch the STS in the early 1980s, increasing the number of missions and lobbying for more financial support from Congress—all the while projecting a slick public image of almost casual achievement. In 1982 NASA projected an optimistic schedule: 12 launches in 1984 (there were only four); 14 in 1985 (eight); 17 in 1986 and 1987; and thereafter 24 each year—or one every two weeks. Such a schedule actually seemed possible when in 1983 the second shuttle orbiter, *Challenger,* made its debut, followed in 1984 by *Discovery,* and in 1985, *Atlantis*. Obviously it would be difficult to achieve such a loaded flight schedule, but NASA had promised "routine access to space" and was pushing itself hard to live up to that promise.

Teacher
in Space

The crew of *Challenger* mission 51-L poses in the White Room of launchpad 39B: from left to right: payload specialists Christa McAuliffe and Gregory B. Jarvis, mission specialist Judith A. Resnik, Commander Francis R. Scobee, mission specialist Ronald E. McNair, pilot Michael J. Smith, and mission specialist Ellison Onizuka.

By the mid-1970s, with the STS still in initial stages of development, the number of active astronauts had dropped to 27. Looking for members to crew the new space shuttle, NASA announced a call for astronauts in July 1976, encouraging women and minorities to apply.

Just as the design of the shuttle drastically changed from that of earlier spacecrafts, the requirements for astronaut crew members changed, too. Because the force of reentry would be only 3 g (three times the force of Earth's gravity) instead of 8 g, certain physical fitness requirements were relaxed. The crew area of the shuttle was much bigger, too, than the Apollo command modules. The shuttle could carry as many as six or seven crew members, including a new type of astronaut—"the mission specialist."

Although not trained as pilots, mission specialists had to have bachelor's degrees in engineering, physical science, or math. They also had to be from five feet to six feet four inches in height. Unlike the Apollo astronauts, whose physical size was limited by the dimensions of the command module, the size of the shuttle astronauts was limited only by the technology of the EVA suits, worn for space walks. The shuttle suits were bigger than the Apollo ones and could accommodate a greater range of height. Mission specialist applicants, like all other astronaut candidates, had to pass vision and hearing tests, but these tests were less stringent than those required for previous astronauts and pilots. There was no age limit.

Pilot applicants also had to have at least a bachelor's degree in physical science, engineering, or math. And they had to have logged at least 1,000 hours of pilot time, too, although 2,000 hours was preferred. NASA also preferred that these hours had been spent piloting high-performance jets or test vehicles. Pilot applicants had to pass a more rigorous physical examination than that required of mission specialists, and height restrictions ranged from five feet four inches to six feet four inches tall.

By June 1977, NASA received more than 6,300 applications. In the end, 208 candidates were invited for interviews and medical tests. In January 1978 the space agency announced the selection of 35 new astronauts—15 pilots and 20 mission specialists. This group was the first to include women and members of minority groups: six women, three African Americans, and an Asian American. The new astronauts began their training in July. Originally, NASA expected astronaut training to last two years, but discovered it could be completed in one year.

When not flying missions, astronauts are expected to work in supporting roles. One of the most visible jobs is that of the "capcom," the only person in the flight control room in Houston who speaks to the astronauts

during missions. The capcom is always an astronaut. Shuttle astronauts also work on debugging software in the Shuttle Avionics Integration Laboratory, and in payload support (readying the cargo before a mission). Always overachievers, astronauts provide a valuable resource in other areas such as equipment and protocol design. However, when assigned to upcoming missions, they spend much of their time training in flight simulators, water tanks (where practicing underwater allows them to simulate weightlessness), or airplanes (where trainees can experience temporary zero gravity).

NASA soon realized that more astronauts were needed to provide for all these duties plus the planned shuttle missions. So on August 1, 1979, the space agency announced more openings. Of the approximately 3,200 applicants, NASA interviewed 121 candidates and in May

Astronaut trainees prepare for emergency measures to take in case of ejection from aircraft over water. Participating in the 1978 training exercises is Ronald E. McNair, who in 1984 would travel as a mission specialist on the *Challenger*, becoming the second African American to fly in space. In 1985 he would be selected for a second trip into space, once again aboard the *Challenger*.

1980 chose 19 astronauts, including four more women and members of minority groups. Beginning in 1983, and anticipating several missions each year, NASA announced it would interview astronaut applicants every year.

In the fall of 1984, political considerations intruded on the shuttle flight plan. President Reagan initiated a Teacher in Space Project, in which a school teacher would be selected to travel on the space shuttle and teach lessons to children from space. The program would demonstrate Reagan's support for education and tie in with NASA's desire to show how safe shuttle transportation was. Members of the "teacher mission," scheduled as mission 51-L, would fly the shuttle *Challenger*.

Heading the mission was 46-year-old Commander Francis R. "Dick" Scobee, who was one of the group of astronauts selected in 1978. Born in 1939 in Cle Elum, Washington, Scobee enlisted in the U.S. Air Force in 1957 after his high school graduation. Trained as an aircraft mechanic, he enrolled in the University of Arizona in 1963. Two years later, after earning a bachelor's degree in aerospace engineering, Scobee volunteered for flight school and was trained to fly cargo and transport planes.

Dick Scobee served in Vietnam from 1967 to 1969 as a cargo plane pilot. Upon his return to the United States, he was accepted by the Aerospace Research Pilot School at Edwards Air Force Base in California. Completing his studies in 1972, Scobee stayed at Edwards, where he worked as a test pilot. He logged more than 6,500 hours of flight time in 45 different types of test aircraft, including one that was a precursor to the shuttle, the X-24B.

After his selection and training as an astronaut in 1978, Scobee served as backup for the first space shuttle mission. He also flew the NASA Boeing 747 that carried the orbiter back to Kennedy Space Center after it landed in California, and in April 1984 piloted a *Challenger* mission during which a solar satellite was successfully repaired. By proving that in-space repairs were possible, that mission helped win over some critics of manned space flight. Scobee was married and had two children.

The pilot for mission 51-L was 40-year-old Michael J. Smith, from Beaufort, North Carolina. In 1967 Smith earned his bachelor's degree in naval science from the U.S. Naval Academy in Annapolis, Maryland. A year later, he received a master's degree in aeronautical engineering from the Navy Postgraduate School. Smith trained as a pilot and later worked as an instructor at Advanced Jet Training Command.

Like Scobee, Smith served in Vietnam for two years. In 1973, after completing his tour of duty, he studied at the U.S. Navy Test Pilot School, where he later served as a test pilot for two years and as an instructor for a year and a half. He logged more than 4,500 hours of flight time in 28 different aircraft, mostly jets. Smith became an astronaut in May 1980. From 1981, when he completed his training course, to 1985, he worked in a variety of support positions at the space agency. Mission 51-L would be the first space flight for Smith, a father of three.

Mission specialist Ronald E. McNair was assigned to mission 51-L to operate the Spartan-Halley satellite that would observe Halley's comet, whose orbit passes close to earth every 76 years. The 35-year-old African American was born in Lake City, South Carolina, where he excelled as both a student and an athlete, overcoming the institutionalized prejudice of segregation. After graduating from high school in 1967, he earned a bachelor's degree in physics from North Carolina Agricultural and Technical State University in 1971. Five years later, he received a doctorate in physics from the highly regarded Massachusetts Institute of Technology.

McNair's area of expertise was quantum electronics

and laser technology, which he researched at MIT and in France. The multitalented McNair was an author, a black belt in karate, a father of two, and a scientist at Hughes Research Laboratories in California. He applied for the job of astronaut in 1977 and in February 1984 became the second African American to fly in space, on a *Challenger* shuttle mission.

Air force lieutenant colonel Ellison S. Onizuka had become the first Asian American in space when he flew aboard *Discovery* in January 1985. On that classified mission, Onizuka helped deploy a top-secret Department of Defense satellite. The 39-year-old Onizuka was born in Kealakekua, Kona, Hawaii, and graduated from high school in 1964. A member of the Reserve Officers' Training Corps (ROTC) while in school, he received both his bachelor's and master's degrees in aerospace engineering from the University of Colorado at Boulder in 1969, before entering active duty in the U.S. Air Force.

Onizuka was a flight test engineer from 1971 to 1974, when he enrolled in the Air Force Test Pilot School at Edwards Air Force Base. After graduation, Onizuka stayed on at the base as an instructor, logging 1,700 hours on 43 different types of aircraft. Selected by NASA in 1978, Onizuka, like Smith and McNair, served in a variety of positions before being assigned mission specialist to mission 51-L. Also like McNair, Onizuka was married with two children.

The third mission specialist on *Challenger* mission 51-L was 36-year-old Judith A. Resnik. She became the second American woman in space in August 1984, on the first flight of *Discovery*. Born in Akron, Ohio, Resnik graduated from high school in 1966, and earned her bachelor's degree in electrical engineering in 1970 from Carnegie-Mellon University, in Pennsylvania.

Resnik was an engineer for RCA Corporation in

New Jersey and Virginia in the early 1970s; her area of expertise was radar systems and rocket telemetry (the science of detecting and measuring quantitative data such as pressure, speed, and temperature). Then she worked as a biomedical engineer for the National Institutes of Health in Maryland, and in 1977 earned a doctor of philosophy in electrical engineering from the University of Maryland. Resnik worked for a year at the Xerox Corporation in California, and then applied to the astronaut program, which selected her in 1978. Commander Scobee specifically requested Resnik for mission 51-L because of her experience with the shuttle robot arm used to retrieve satellites from orbit. Lively and gregarious, the unmarried Resnik was a favorite of the press.

Along with the commander, pilot, and three mission specialists assigned to mission 51-L were two civilians serving as payload specialists. One was 41-year-old Gregory B. Jarvis. Born in Detroit, Michigan, Jarvis graduated from high school in 1962 and earned a bachelor's degree in electrical engineering at the State University of New York at Buffalo in 1967. He also held two master's degrees—one in electrical engineering from Northeastern University, Boston (1969), and the other in management science from West Coast University in Los Angeles (1986). He and his wife lived in California.

Like Onizuka, Jarvis was an ROTC student in college. In 1969 he began active duty with the Space Division of the U.S. Air Force in California, where he worked for four years on military satellites. After discharge he became an engineer for Hughes Aircraft Corporation. In June 1984, as supervisor of a satellite program, Jarvis was selected by Hughes and NASA to accompany the company's satellite into space. He had originally been assigned to two previous shuttle missions, but lost his place on *Discovery* in April 1985 to Utah Senator Jake Garn, and

Teacher in Space Project

After her selection from more than 11,000 applicants to be a citizen observer and payload specialist for the Teacher in Space Project, Christa McAuliffe (facing page) spent a year in astronaut training. Here, she practices in the zero-gravity environment provided by a specially modified jet aircraft.

in January 1986 on the *Columbia* to Florida congressman William Nelson.

The second payload specialist and final crew member of mission 51-L was schoolteacher Sharon Christa Corrigan McAuliffe. When President Reagan had first announced that a teacher—not a journalist, as had been previously announced—would be the first private citizen in space, McAuliffe had been eager to apply. "I watched the space program being born and I would like to participate," she stated in her application. After a much-publicized search and review of 11,000 applicants for the Teacher in Space Project, NASA narrowed the list to 114 applicants. The selection of the New Hampshire high school teacher from the ten finalists was announced on July 19, 1985, at a White House ceremony.

The 37-year-old Boston, Massachusetts, native graduated from high school in 1966. McAuliffe earned a bachelor of arts degree from Framingham State College, Massachusetts, in 1970, and a master's in education from Bowie State College, Maryland, in 1978. She also taught junior high school in Maryland from 1970 until 1978, and taught at other schools in New Hampshire when she and her husband moved there. At the time of her selection for the Teacher in Space Project, McAuliffe was teaching economics, law, and history at Concord High School, in Concord, New Hampshire.

Even astronauts and other NASA personnel, who might have been expected to be a little resentful of this "amateur," liked McAuliffe for her straightforwardness, enthusiasm, and complete lack of arrogance. There was some annoyance that the scientific goals of the mission, and even the presence of six other highly

trained specialists on the flight, were often ignored by the media, which focused on the teacher in the mission. Still, McAuliffe was a public-relations masterpiece for NASA and for President Reagan.

Christa McAuliffe soon became a national idol. Her purpose on mission 51-L was to record the experiences of astronaut training and space flight and to communicate her experiences with others, particularly school children. During the flight McAuliffe was scheduled to teach two lessons from space.

Like her fellow crew members, McAuliffe would have several important spectators with her at Kennedy Space Center. Her husband, two children, parents, and several of her students would be in the viewing stands, watching *Challenger* launch.

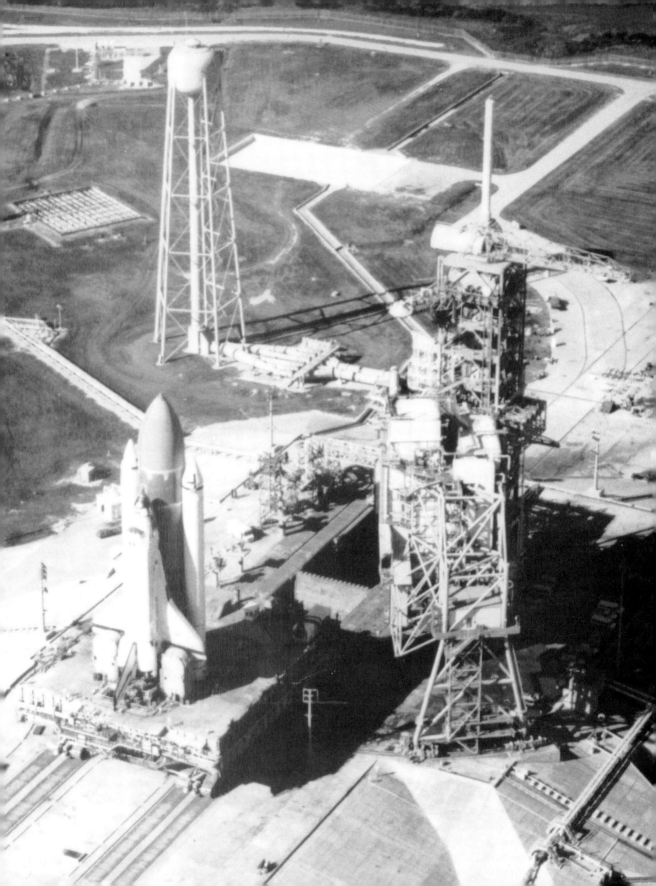

In December 1985 space shuttle *Challenger* was moved to newly renovated launchpad B after a 3.5-mile journey from the Vehicle Assembly Building. Although the shuttle's liftoff was initially planned for that month, launch would be postponed to January.

The Night Before

Thousands of workers at NASA worked full-time to prepare for each shuttle mission—indeed, hundreds at Kennedy Space Center alone just for each launch—but with so many flights on the schedule, it became hard to keep up. Soon delays set the program back, while NASA strove to meet the goal of faster turnaround between missions. Employees worked 75 and even 80 hours per week. Inevitably, there were some people who had to be in three places at once. Exhaustion and overwork affects even the most dedicated workers, and can lead to serious mistakes in almost any job, but it is particularly dangerous in a space program.

In December 1985, the space shuttle *Columbia* came back from a two-year overhaul, but its launch was scrubbed (canceled) an unprecedented seven times due to bad weather conditions or mechanical problems. Critics dubbed the planned flight "Mission Impossible" until it finally launched on January 12, with Congressman William Nelson aboard. Nelson was the chair of the U.S. House Space Science and Applications Committee, which approved NASA's budget.

Columbia's launch enabled Kennedy technicians to finally focus on *Challenger*'s upcoming Teacher in Space flight—at least for a few days. The delays with *Columbia* threatened the schedule for all subsequent shuttle missions. *Columbia* was to return on January 18, and *Challenger*'s launch had been scheduled for January 22, just a few days later. During the month before *Challenger*'s scheduled liftoff date, NASA was simultaneously preparing for three separate missions, and personnel were overworked. In the 27 days before mission 51-L was to launch, not one key technician at Kennedy Space Center had had any time off.

Because budget constraints restricted the number of spare parts available for the orbiters, technicians would borrow components from one orbiter to use on another— a practice known as cannibalization. This is not the safest option, since every time a part is moved, no matter how careful one is, there is a chance of damage. Because of the shortage of parts, NASA could keep only two of its four orbiters in the air at the same time. Launching a shuttle with cannibalized parts, NASA believed, was preferable to having it grounded and not earning its keep.

Columbia was cannibalized almost as soon as it landed in California; the removed parts included sensors and a computer. *Challenger* also borrowed parts from *Discovery* and *Atlantis*—a situation not made public at the time.

Why not just postpone mission 51-L? Actually, the shuttle schedule had already been altered. Because of delays in the *Columbia* mission, *Challenger*'s liftoff had

been pushed back to January 23, and then January 24. Launch was reset for January 25 and then rescheduled to January 27, and then was delayed yet another 24 hours because of problems with the orbiter hatch. But the launch schedule for the year was packed, and many of the missions were time-sensitive.

Mission 51-L was no less important and perhaps more time-sensitive than many. It was to launch a Tracking Data Relay Satellite (TDRS), which would allow NASA to maintain continuous contact with its orbiters; the existing system relied on numerous earth stations, which resulted in periodic communication blackouts. The mission was also to deploy the Spartan-Halley satellite, which would be used to observe Halley's comet.

After mission 51-L, *Columbia* was scheduled for another launch on March 6, six weeks later, also to

Columbia touches down on the dry lake-bed runway at Edwards Air Force Base in southern California. After the orbiter returned from its January 12–18 flight, some of its parts were removed and installed on the *Challenger*. Because of NASA's budgetary constraints, such cannibalization of parts was common at the time.

With temperatures forecast to drop to the teens on the night before *Challenger*'s launch, personnel left the water running in the launch pad pipes to prevent them from freezing. In the extreme cold, the water drains soon froze shut, and by dawn frost and stalactites of ice encrusted equipment (above) and engulfed the launch tower (facing page).

observe Halley's comet before it traveled too far away from earth. Then on May 15, *Challenger* was scheduled to launch again, this time carrying a controversial payload—the Centaur rocket, to be used in deploying a satellite to observe Jupiter and the sun. The Centaur rocket carried liquid fuel, which is much more volatile than the more customary solid fuel, and it also contained plutonium, a radioactive element. Carrying such materials in its hold, the orbiter would be like a huge bomb. NASA had opposed the use of liquid fuel in the Centaur rocket, but had been overruled by General Dynamics, the contractor that made the rocket.

Unusually low temperatures were forecast for the night before *Challenger*'s January 28 launch, so all the water pipes and faucets on the launch pad were set at a trickle to keep the pipes from freezing. Normally NASA required that the entire water system be drained whenever the temperatures fell below 32°F, but neither the time nor the money for such an operation was available. As an added precaution against the cold weather, antifreeze was poured all over the pad, especially under the solid rocket boosters.

The low temperatures presented another problem. The previous day technicians responsible for filling the external tank with liquid oxygen (which remains in liquid form only at extremely low temperatures) had discovered that the ET vent temperature was lower than NASA's required limit of 45°F. The vent, which allowed gases boiling off from the liquid fuel to escape, would normally be warmed by an electric heater. But with the freezing outside temperatures and the cold of the liquid fuel, the heater was not working properly. In response to this problem, NASA had already issued a waiver, lowering the acceptable temperature limit for the vent to 28°F. But on the eve of the launch, as technicians prepared to fill the huge external tank with liquid fuel, they discovered that the temperature of the vent had fallen further, this time to 24°F. So NASA changed its acceptable limit yet again, this time to 10°F. An outsider might wonder about the point of setting safety regulations if they could be so easily circumvented.

In the middle of the night, an ice team inspected the launch pad. Normally the team would ensure that any ice, which often formed on the external tank, would not damage the orbiter tiles. This time, however, NASA inspectors were dumbfounded to see that the trickling water

from the open pipes had accumulated and frozen, leaving layers of ice covering the west and north sides of the tower, with some icicles as long as 18 inches. Several inches of ice encased the crew access arm, the emergency escape route for the astronauts. The situation was dangerous, because in the event the crew needed to exit the orbiter quickly, they could fall on the slippery surface. Possible damage to the heat tiles was also a concern. It was hoped that conditions would improve by dawn.

One hour before the astronauts were due to board, the ice team went out again and found the pad in even worse condition. After they reported their findings to management, the program manager from Houston,

Arnold Aldrich, pushed back the launch time from 9:38 A.M. to 11:38 A.M. This would allow for a third inspection, for personnel to remove most of the ice from the pad, and for the ice to melt if the temperature warmed up. If a morning liftoff was not possible, there was another launch window from 3 P.M. to 6 P.M. that day.

Yet another concern was the effect of the freezing temperatures on the solid rocket booster joints and on the O-rings that held the joints in place. There had been trouble with Morton Thiokol's SRB joint design even before it was approved in 1980 and during *Columbia*'s second flight in November 1981, but the story did not end there. Engineers at Marshall Space Flight Center were aware that joint rotation, resulting in gas blow-by and O-ring erosion, had occurred several times in subsequent shuttle flights. Marshall officials had said nothing about the problem to the other NASA control centers, believing the issue was within their jurisdiction and under control.

However it was clear that the O-rings were essential to the safe operation of the boosters. After *Columbia*'s second flight, NASA had designated both the primary and secondary O-rings as "Criticality 1," meaning that their failure could cause loss of life. Both were necessary to prevent joint rotation. However, the agency did not stop the shuttle flights in order to fix the booster joint design flaw that was causing the O-ring erosion.

In 1982, NASA accepted bids from various aerospace companies for building new, lighter boosters. Morton Thiokol had submitted its same design for the booster joints. Another company, Hercules Inc., had submitted a new design that solved the problem of joint rotation and hence O-ring erosion. Hercules was awarded the contract in May 1982, and the first boosters using the new joint design were to be tested in July 1986. NASA could have retooled the old boosters to use the new joint design, but

that would have cost time and money, and added weight to the shuttle. NASA did make the casings (walls) of the SRBs slightly thinner, reflecting the new design, which ended up exacerbating the heavy stress on the old, thicker-design joints.

During subsequent shuttle flights, O-ring erosion continued to occur. After a February 1984 mission, more scorched O-rings were discovered. A month later, a Marshall system report acknowledged the "[p]ossibility exists for some O-ring erosion on future flights. . . . [T]his is not a constraint to future launches." Testing had shown the erosion that occurred was an acceptable risk. Technicians had cut away three times as much of the O-rings as had eroded, and then tested their effectiveness in the boosters.

A close-up of the top of an SRB segment. The SRBs were made up of steel segments connected at specially designed joints held in place by O-rings. Some engineers were concerned that freezing temperatures would affect the SRB joints, which had already demonstrated problems during shuttle flights.

The 1984 system report showed that the erosion and scorching of a component that was not even supposed to come in direct contact with extreme heat was being accepted as normal wear and tear.

During a January 1985 shuttle flight, a primary O-ring burned completely through, and the secondary O-ring just barely held. This flight had launched when the outside temperature was 53°F, the coldest launch temperature for shuttle missions to date. When NASA discovered the burn-through, the agency asked Morton Thiokol for a complete review. The following month Thiokol replied that the cold temperature had been a factor in causing the erosion, but the contractor did not recommend a suspension of launches. The condition was deemed acceptable.

On an April 1985 shuttle flight, an O-ring burned through, and the secondary ring also eroded, but still functioned. After this incident, booster project manager Lawrence Mulloy of the Marshall Space Flight Center issued a "launch constraint" until Marshall could fix the O-ring erosion problem, or at the very least double-check the joints before each launch. Although this prohibition took effect six months before the Teacher in Space Project was to launch, Mulloy approved all subsequent launches by writing and signing waivers—thus keeping missions on schedule.

In July 1985, the Marshall Space Flight Center ordered 72 new booster segments from Morton Thiokol, although the new segments were to be made according to the Hercules company's design. In the meantime, NASA proposed to continue flights using the old booster joint design. That same month, Thiokol engineer Roger Boisjoly wrote to his boss that the O-ring erosion was a serious problem and the joints had a basic design flaw.

But Morton Thiokol management resisted efforts to make any changes. On August 19, 1985, Thiokol officials briefed the Marshall senior managers about O-ring erosion but gave the impression that although the problem was serious, it could be resolved. Still, no one at Morton Thiokol or Marshall issued a launch veto for any shuttle flights. Although the contractor appointed a special "seal team," headed by Roger Boisjoly, to focus on the booster joint problem, the company did not support the team. Morton Thiokol was in the running for another NASA contract and was reluctant to admit a basic design flaw.

At the end of the year, in December 1985, Morton Thiokol formally requested that NASA declare the problem with O-rings closed. On January 23, 1986, just five days before *Challenger* would finally launch, the issue was officially closed at Marshall Space Flight Center. As Mulloy explained, "Since the risk of O-ring erosion was accepted and indeed expected, it was no longer considered an anomaly to be resolved before the next flight."

On the night of January 27, 1986, when freezing temperatures were forecast for eastern Florida, one NASA manager remembered that the SRBs were said to not perform very well at low temperatures. Just to be safe, Larry Wear, Marshall's solid rocket motor manager, contacted the Morton Thiokol engineers at their facility in Utah to see what they thought about the effect of the forecasted temperatures on the SRBs.

At a teleconference held among management and engineers from Kennedy Space Center, Marshall Space Flight Center, and Morton Thiokol, the contractor's representatives discussed the effect of cold on the SRB joints. The engineers would later acknowledge that because some of the worst O-ring erosion had occurred during a launch held at 75°F, they did not present their case very convincingly. Nevertheless Thiokol engineers unanimously recommended against launch unless the temperature was at least 53°F.

NASA officials challenged that recommendation—such an action was not unusual in engineering circles, and certainly not in meetings between the agency and its contractors. After all, the shuttle was designed for year-round use. NASA officials pointed out that Morton Thiokol hadn't mentioned any potential problems with the launch temperature the day before (when *Challenger* was previously scheduled to launch), when it was only 40°F. Thiokol personnel then asked for a few moments to discuss the issue among themselves.

Meanwhile NASA personnel prepared themselves mentally to call off the launch. Many at the space agency expected Morton Thiokol to come back with more information to solidify its recommendation not to launch. The deputy director of science and engineering at Marshall, George Hardy, disagreed with the engineers' advice. But he did say, "I will not agree to launch against the contractor's recommendation." So those in the room at NASA were prepared to start making some phone calls. Postponing a launch was a massive operation, and countless employees had to be found and notified.

After about 30 minutes, Morton Thiokol engineers came back on the line to announce that they had changed their minds and would allow the launch. What NASA officials did not know was that there was no more information for the contractor to present, and some personnel at Morton Thiokol had felt pressured to recommend a launch. The fact was, they did not have enough hard evidence that the O-rings would not function properly in cold weather.

In the early morning hours before the launch, NASA received another contractor's warning to call off the flight. Rockwell International, the company responsible for building the orbiter, warned NASA that the ice on the launch pad might damage the orbiter's heat-resistant tiles or other equipment, or could even be aspirated (sucked in) by the SRBs during liftoff. Rockwell believed it was not safe to launch, and noted it "could not assure it was safe to fly." NASA officials decided it was.

By the time *Challenger* was to launch, the ambient temperature was 36°F. However, the temperatures of the rocket boosters were even lower. The left-hand SRB, sitting in the sun, was about 25°F and the right-hand SRB, which was in the shade, was 8°F.

After lengthy delays and several postponements, the space shuttle *Challenger*, with a crew of seven astronauts aboard, lifts off from pad 39B at 11:38 A.M. on January 28, 1986.

"Obviously a Major Malfunction"

January 28, 1986
Kennedy Space Center, Florida

The day dawned clear and unusually cold on the morning of the launch of mission 51-L. At 11:29 A.M. the final nine-minute countdown began.

The astronauts' families watched from a safe distance at a special NASA viewing stand. They listened to a NASA information officer's voice over a loudspeaker, and they could hear some of the transmissions between launch control and Commander Dick Scobee and pilot Mike Smith. Finally, at T minus six seconds, the orbiter's engines fired up; then the solid rocket boosters ignited. The *Challenger* lifted off the pad atop a huge fireball and billowing smoke and steam. The crowd cheered.

As the viewers watched and listened, Commander Scobee prepared to roll the *Challenger* over so that its payload doors faced the earth. Then Scobee decreased the engine power slightly in order to pass through a thicker, turbulent layer of atmosphere. Once through the layer, at T plus 1:00 (one minute after launch), NASA control radioed the shuttle commander to return to full power: "Go at throttle up." Scobee responded "Roger, go at throttle up." Then NASA ground control heard Mike Smith's voice: "Uh-oh!"

Challenger's external tank burst open in midair, spraying debris for thousands of feet around it. The two solid rocket boosters separated and shot off in different directions. Huge puffs of what looked like smoke (it was actually evaporating gas) billowed from what used to be the shuttle. The cloud was so huge and far away that nobody could see what had happened to the orbiter and its crew. The families of the astronauts and other spectators, including some of McAuliffe's students, stared upward in disbelief. For a few seconds, the loudspeaker continued to announce the spacecraft's height and velocity—the mission control announcer in Houston had no television monitors, only data screens. Then there was a long pause. Finally the voice said,

> Flight controllers here looking very carefully at the situation. Obviously a major malfunction. We have no downlink [no communications link with the crew]. We have a report from the flight dynamics officer that the vehicle has exploded. The flight director confirms that. We are looking at checking with the recovery forces to see what can be done at this point.

Spectators prayed silently for a parachute, an escape pod, anything. But NASA had long known that the first

two minutes of a shuttle mission were the most danger-ous. From the time that the SRBs ignited just before launch until they were jettisoned, there was no way for the crew to escape should anything go wrong. The 25th space shuttle mission was the worst disaster in the history of space exploration. It had lasted 73 seconds.

NASA officials immediately dispatched ships to the approximate site of the orbiter's impact. It soon became clear that no one had survived, though it was hoped that the crew members had died quickly and painlessly. Any crack or puncture in the walls of the orbiter cabin would have resulted in a rapid depressurization that would have caused the crew to pass out within 15 to 18 seconds.

That night, President Ronald Reagan postponed his scheduled State of the Union address and instead consoled

Just 73 seconds after launch, *Challenger* explodes, marking the sky with gas and conden-sation from the main engine exhaust, solid rocket boosters, and the external tank. The two white plumes indicate where the twin rocket boosters separated.

a shocked nation. His address recognized the pain of the millions of schoolchildren who had eagerly followed the Teacher in Space Project, and who had witnessed the disaster live on television. In his closing statement, he quoted from the sonnet "High Flight," written by John Gillespie Magee, a Canadian pilot killed during World War II:

> The crew of the space shuttle *Challenger* honored us by the manner in which they lived their lives. We will never forget them, nor the last time we saw them, this morning, as they prepared for their journey and waved goodbye, and "slipped the surly bonds of Earth to touch the face of God."

For some time after the *Challenger* explosion, nobody knew what had gone wrong. One reason was that it had happened so quickly—and since the shuttle was four miles from the launch pad by then, no one on the ground could determine what happened. Before the breakup, even the astronauts aboard the shuttle did not realize anything was amiss. The key events of the disaster occurred not in seconds, but in tenths and hundredths of seconds. The recovery operation and the search for shuttle debris, on the other hand, would last for seven months.

After extensive analysis of all the photos, recordings, telemetry data, and salvaged pieces that NASA could collect, investigators determined the precise sequence of events. Just before launch, a large puff of black smoke escaped from the back joint of the right-hand solid rocket booster. Soot and debris sealed the joint temporarily, but at 58.7 seconds, a flame appeared in the side of the right SRB. The flame grew larger and burned at 6,000°F near the strut that attached the SRB to the external tank. The ET, filled with liquid hydrogen and oxygen, was highly sensitive to heat—rather like an enormous bomb.

Spectators at Kennedy Space Center quickly realize that something has gone very wrong with *Challenger*'s launch. Millions more across the nation, who had been following the launch of the Teacher in Space mission on television—at homes and in classrooms—reacted in shock and disbelief.

At that moment *Challenger* approached the layer of atmosphere nine miles in the sky known as "max Q," where speed and aerodynamic pressure place the greatest amount of stress on an aircraft. NASA ground controllers could read the shuttle's telemetry data, but only later realized its significance: heavy wind gusts were buffeting the shuttle, causing it to experience a violent wind shear. The severe shaking weakened the strut anchoring the leaking booster.

Then events occurred almost simultaneously. The strut gave way. The solid rocket booster swung free and the external tank burst open from the pressure of burning hydrogen and oxygen. Pushed by the force of the escaping gas, the SRB sheared off the right wing of *Challenger*. Then the entire shuttle exploded, breaking up the orbiter. A shower of debris fell at varying speeds across the brilliant blue sky. Some of it seemed to take an eternity to fall. A military field safety officer detonated the SRBs, which were still burning, to prevent them from crashing into a populated area.

After extensive analysis of flight data, it became clear that pilot Michael Smith uttered, "Uh-oh!" just before the strut broke. It is theorized that he saw on his data screen that the right SRB was suffering a loss of pressure. To compensate, the left SRB was working extra hard to keep the shuttle stable, as were the shuttle's main engines. Commander Scobee opened up a communications link, but before he could speak, communication was cut off by the massive explosion.

After two months of intensive searching, the crew compartment of the orbiter was discovered under 100 feet of water. By that time, there was no longer any way to tell if the crew cabin had been intact after the orbiter breakup. Searchers did not find all seven emergency oxygen packs, but of the packs they did find all but one had been activated. It was clear that at least a few of the astronauts had remained conscious long enough to activate their oxygen packs.

Investigators estimated that the crew cabin took from two to three minutes to fall into the Atlantic Ocean, which meant it would have hit the water at a speed of over 200 miles per hour. If the crew members survived the breakup, they could have been conscious when the cabin hit the water. Investigators did say that all seven crew members were strapped into their seats when found—so it is likely they passed out during the three-minute fall.

The astronauts' bodies were recovered in April and released to their families at the end of the month. On May 20, two of the crew members, Scobee and Smith, were buried at Arlington National Cemetery, where a Shuttle *Challenger* Memorial was also placed.

The aftermath of the *Challenger* disaster differed from that of the *Apollo 1* fire, when NASA sealed off its launch center from the press and formed its own internal review board. Instead, after *Challenger*, NASA released a great deal of information to the public. President Reagan appointed a Presidential Commission, headed by former secretary of state William Rogers, to investigate the cause or causes of the accident and formulate recommendations for NASA. President Reagan told NASA that its personnel had to follow the Commission's recommendations to the letter and provide ongoing reports on its progress. Commission members included astronauts Neil Armstrong and Sally Ride, test pilot Chuck Yeager, and a number of other illustrious professionals.

After holding hearings from February 6 to May 2, the Presidential Commission released its 256-page report on the space shuttle *Challenger* accident on June 6, 1986. It found that faulty O-ring seals on the right-hand solid rocket booster had caused the explosion of the *Challenger* on its January 28 flight. But the Commission also found fault with NASA and Morton Thiokol for failing to acknowledge previous problems with the design of the SRB joints and for failing to adequately test O-rings and joints at low temperatures.

Besides targeting these mechanical and technological failures, the Commission's report also blamed NASA management. The Commission faulted Marshall Space Flight Center for attempting to resolve serious problems

Two segments of a solid rocket booster are examined by investigators of the space shuttle *Challenger* explosion. Former secretary of state and attorney general William P. Rogers (facing page) headed the Presidential Commission investigating the *Challenger* accident.

internally instead of informing other centers of its concerns. Those outside NASA, including the Commissioners, were shocked to learn that the 25th space shuttle launch was approved even though 14 of the previous 24 successful shuttle missions had produced evidence of damage to the SRB seals. Improved communications between the separate flight centers was paramount.

Richard Feynman, a noted scientist and member of the Presidential Commission, remarked on the statement made during the investigation by NASA senior management that shuttle flights had a 1 in 100,000

chance of failure: "Since one part in 100,000 would imply that one could launch a shuttle each day for 300 years expecting to lose only one . . . [i]t would appear that, for whatever purpose—be it for internal or external consumption—the management of NASA exaggerates the reliability of its product to the point of fantasy." NASA engineers and technicians, however, more familiar with the "product" than their managers, routinely placed the odds closer to one in 1,000, even as low as one in 300.

Another public comment by Professor Feynman was quoted in the Commission's report and often in newspapers. According to Feynman, the decision making at NASA was "a kind of Russian roulette. . . . [The shuttle] flies [with O-ring erosion] and nothing happens. Then it is suggested, therefore, that the risk is no longer so high for the next flights. We can lower our standards a little bit because we got away with it last time." NASA, it appeared to many Americans, was gambling with the astronauts' lives.

Astronaut John Young agreed. A veteran of the Gemini and Apollo programs and the first commander of a space shuttle flight, Young sent a memo to senior NASA management, and copies to all other astronauts. In it, he criticized NASA's willingness to compromise safety: "There is only one driving reason that a potentially dangerous system would be allowed to fly: launch schedule pressure." Astronauts were particularly appalled that they had not known of problems with the space shuttle seals and joints, even though design flaws had been discovered before the spacecraft ever flew.

Regarding the many, many problems that were discovered in the shuttle system after the accident, Young declared, "On an individual basis, they were not big enough to slow or stop the launch rates. But totally, this list is awesome. The list proves to me that there are some very lucky people around here."

The Commission made several other recommendations. A redesign of SRB joints, of course, topped the list, but so did development of safer, expendable boosters, rather than reusable ones. The Commission also wanted NASA to investigate the development of escape systems that would be available immediately after launch, during controlled gliding flight, and during emergency runway landings. NASA was told to find a higher safety margin for landing procedures, as well, by improving the orbiter tire, brake, and nose-wheel systems.

The Commission recommended the establishment of a safety office and an independent oversight committee, and the promotion of qualified astronauts into NASA management positions. The space agency was also required to review its testing and maintenance procedures, paying special attention to Criticality 1 components, whose failure could be fatal to astronauts. Perhaps the most notable recommendation, however, indicated that NASA should reduce the number of shuttle missions: "NASA must establish a flight rate that is consistent with its resources."

William Rogers himself did not recommend that criminal charges be brought against anyone involved. Others did—Senator Ernest Hollings said that Lawrence Mulloy's behavior as manager of Marshall's SRB project constituted "gross negligence," and that Marshall Space Flight Center director William Lucas "showed no remorse, no misgivings, no understanding of individual responsibility." The two men claimed that if they had known about the teleconference held on January 27 they would not have approved the launch. In effect, Hollings felt, they blamed their subordinates.

At NASA—like any corporation where a major error is made—heads rolled. Several NASA and Morton Thiokol senior officials resigned, were transferred, or were fired. NASA administrator James Beggs, who had been on leave from the agency since December 1985, resigned in February 1986. He was replaced in May by former NASA head James Fletcher, the man who in the early 1970s had helped the agency obtain the funding for the space shuttle system. Fletcher would oversee NASA's recovery from the *Challenger* disaster, from 1986 to 1989.

The Shuttle Program Office director, Jesse Moore, resigned, and an astronaut, Richard Truly, took his place. It was the first time an astronaut was placed in a senior management position. Truly would later become the administrator of NASA itself, from 1989 to 1992. Future critical launch decisions made by the Shuttle Program Office became the responsibility of astronaut Robert Crippen, who later became the director of Kennedy Space Center.

The president of Morton Thiokol took early retirement, and his vice president transferred to another division. Supervisor Robert Lund, who at first supported his engineers and then changed his mind, was transferred. The director of the Solid Rocket Motor Project at Morton Thiokol, Alan McDonald, who had protested the launch because of concerns about the cold weather, was promoted to SRB division manager. McDonald reportedly said the night before the launch, "I certainly wouldn't want to be the one that has to get up in front of a board of inquiry if anything happens . . . and explain why I launched the thing." Morton Thiokol took a $10 million loss and agreed to cover the expenses for SRB joint redesign and hardware replacement, at a cost estimated at $505 million.

Thiokol engineer Roger Boisjoly, like Apollo program head Joseph Shea many years before, took the disaster personally. He suffered from post-traumatic stress disorder, a psychological reaction marked by depression, anxiety, and nightmares—a disorder mostly seen in combat veterans. Boisjoly left the company and sued his former employer, but the suit was rejected in September 1988. He vowed never to work for an aerospace company again.

Meanwhile, among the astronaut families, all was not forgotten. The light punishments meted out to NASA and Morton Thiokol decision makers particularly upset those who had lost a loved one in the disaster. Michael Smith's widow sued NASA for $15 million. Betty Grissom, widow of Apollo astronaut Gus Grissom, urged all the families to sue, remarking bitterly that NASA and its contractors didn't care about them. The lawsuit was settled out of court because the government was eager to avoid a public trial, and Morton Thiokol paid a large chunk of the settlements—an undisclosed amount estimated at $2 to $3.5 million per family.

In his memo to NASA senior management following the *Challenger* disaster, astronaut John Young had emphasized the importance of NASA's astronauts to the whole of the space program: "The space program will only succeed in the future if competent and highly qualified men and women who fly the shuttle have confidence in the system." In the aftermath of the accident, several astronauts resigned from NASA. John Young accepted a promotion in April 1987 that took him off active duty. Astronaut Sally Ride wrote an analysis of the direction of the space program. It was made public, but NASA seemed not to heed its advice and Ride resigned.

The technical problems that had caused the *Challenger* explosion were relatively easy to identify and fix. The larger problems were not so easy, and studying them has led some sociologists, journalists, and others to refer to "the *Challenger* Syndrome." This phrase calls to mind the difficulty of unraveling a bureaucratic system that seems to be doing everything "by the book" but still experiences a disaster. The problem was bigger than malfunctioning parts. It lay in corporate culture. Author Claus Jensen lists the difficult questions asked by investigators and the public after the disaster:

> Why did they fly at all with a joint which they knew to be problematic? Why did the subcontractors not listen to their own engineers? And why, later on, did NASA ignore its subcontractors' warnings? Why did they belittle the risk? And why were the people at the top and the bottom of the various organizations living in

One year after the explosion of the *Challenger,* a section of the orbiter is lowered into an abandoned missile silo at Cape Canaveral Air Force Station, in Florida. Two silos at the station serve as permanent storage sites for *Challenger* debris.

such totally different worlds when it came to evaluating the risk involved?

Jensen and other authors believe that NASA is not entirely to blame—the pressure to launch the space shuttles resulted from demands of the American people and Congress who wanted an economical space program. But in a technological field like space flight, economy often results in decreased safety.

On the first anniversary of the *Challenger* disaster, January 28, 1987, silence was observed for 73 seconds at all NASA centers. On that day, 120 tons of *Challenger* salvage were sealed in abandoned missile silos at Cape Canaveral Air Force Station, in Florida.

After the Presidential Commission's recommendations were made public in June 1986, NASA worked to respond to them. In July 1987 the space agency issued its report on the year's activities, addressing each of the Commission's recommendations in turn:

A joint redesign team and advisory panel, consisting of personnel from several NASA centers and industries, and including astronauts, was formed. The National Research Council (NRC) created an independent oversight group. Sam Phillips, former Apollo Program director, was brought in to study the overhauling of the shuttle program organization. Along with this effort, astronaut Robert Crippen also directed a group that investigated communications among the various NASA centers and management levels.

A safety office was formed, which reviewed, among other things, the number of workers required in the program to ensure safe flights. Shuttle components were reviewed in detail and were either recertified for safe flight or redesigned.

Landing safety systems and procedures, already in development at the time of the disaster, were also improved. A new brake system was developed, and NASA canceled future shuttle landings at Kennedy Space Center, opting for the safer facility at Edwards Air Force Base in California. A new, stricter maintenance program was introduced, requiring a larger staff.

Although the launch pad itself had nothing to do with the cause of the disaster, 138 modifications, which cost about $50 million, were made to Pad A. The changes

On May 9, 1991, a memorial to astronauts who have died in the line of duty was dedicated at Kennedy Space Center. Part of the inscription on the black marble slab echoes the words of *Apollo I* astronaut Gus Grissom, "The conquest of space is worth the risk of life."

included ways to avoid the buildup of ice in freezing weather. In the meantime, Pad B was prepared for when the next space shuttle returned to service.

Under the leadership of James Fletcher, NASA launched no shuttles for more than two and a half years. In the meantime, the agency worked to ensure the program's safety and reliability, redesign the solid rocket booster, and restructure its management system. On September 29, 1988, *Discovery* flew the first space shuttle mission since the loss of *Challenger*.

Today, NASA remains a huge organization with

centers across the country and contractors around the world. Tens of thousands of NASA personnel have dedicated their considerable skills to making every mission a success. In 1989, nine shuttle flights were planned, but technicians balked at the schedule and only five flew. Congress provided funds for a replacement orbiter, the *Endeavour*, which first flew in 1992. Since 1988, space shuttles have flown more than 70 missions without a mishap.

Mission safety remains NASA's top concern. Each shuttle launch receives extreme scrutiny and includes numerous safety checks. Whenever anything appears out of the ordinary, NASA does not hesitate to postpone a mission—even a heavily publicized one like the historic 100th shuttle flight, first scheduled to lift off on October 5, 2000. *Discovery*'s launch was scrubbed four times before it finally blasted off on October 11. Mechanical engineer Jorge Rivera, whose debris-inspection team usually checks for ice on the external tank, received credit for two of the four launch scrubs—one due to incomplete retraction of a bolt on the external tank (discovered when Rivera reviewed film from a previous launch of *Atlantis*) and the other because of a 4-inch pin he saw wedged against *Discovery*'s fuel tank (found when he examined the outside of the shuttle with binoculars).

At Kennedy Space Center stands a memorial to all of the American astronauts who have lost their lives in the line of duty. The "Space Mirror" consists of a huge wall of polished black granite blocks; inside the blocks, written in clear glass, are the names of fallen astronauts. The monument moves so that it always faces the sun. When the sun rays hit the wall's polished black surface, the names of America's space heroes are written in the sky.

Chronology

1957   *October 4:* Soviet Union launches first artificial earth satellite, *Sputnik I*

November 3: Soviet Union launches *Sputnik II*, which carries a dog, Laika

1958   *January 31:* United States launches first satellite, *Explorer I*

July: Eisenhower signs the National Aeronautics and Space Act, creating the National Aeronautics and Space Administration (NASA); first American manned space flight program, Project Mercury, is initiated

1959   *April:* NASA announces selection of first seven astronauts for Project Mercury

1961   *April 12:* USSR cosmonaut Yury A. Gagarin becomes first man in space aboard *Vostok 1*

May 5: Alan B. Shepard becomes first American in space during suborbital flight on *Freedom 7*

May 25: President John F. Kennedy declares goal of sending men to the moon

July 21: Gus Grissom becomes second American in space during flight aboard *Liberty Bell 7*

1962   *February 20:* John Glenn makes first U.S. manned orbital flight

1965   *March 23:* Gus Grissom and John Young fly first manned Gemini flight

June 3: James McDivitt and Ed White fly Gemini 4 mission during which White becomes first American to walk in space

1967   *January 27:* Apollo astronauts Gus Grissom, Ed White, and Roger Chaffee perish in the *Apollo 1* fire at Kennedy Space Center, Florida

April 23: Cosmonaut Vladimir Komarov perishes on *Soyuz 1*

1969   *July 20:* *Apollo 11* commander Neil Armstrong is first human to walk on moon

1971   *June 6:* Cosmonauts Georgi Dobrovolsky, Vladislav Volkov, and Viktor Patsayev perish on reentry in *Soyuz 11*

Chronology

1972   *December 19:* Last Apollo lunar landing mission; *Apollo 17* returns from the moon

1977   *February 18: Enterprise*, the U.S. shuttle orbiter, takes its first test flight launched from a Boeing 747 jet

1981   *April 12–14:* First orbital test flight of U.S. space shuttle, *Columbia*, with astronauts John Young and Robert Crippen

1986   *January 28: Challenger* explodes, killing all seven crew members aboard

1988   *September 29: Discovery* flies the space shuttle's first mission since the *Challenger* disaster

2000   *October 11:* NASA's 100th successful shuttle launch takes place, after being postponed several times to ensure mission safety

Bibliography

BOOKS

Bond, Peter. *Heroes in Space: From Gagarin to Challenger.* Oxford, England: B. Blackwell, 1987.

Casamayou, Maureen Hogan. *Bureaucracy in Crisis: Three Mile Island, the Shuttle Challenger, and Risk Assessment.* Boulder, Colo.: Westview Press, 1993.

Cassutt, Michael. *Who's Who in Space: The First 25 Years.* Boston: G. K. Hall, 1987.

Chaikin, Andrew. *A Man on the Moon: The Voyages of the Apollo Astronauts.* New York: Viking, 1994.

Feynman, Richard. *What Do You Care What Other People Think?* New York: Bantam, 1988.

Jensen, Claus. *No Downlink: A Dramatic Narrative About the* Challenger *Accident and Our Time.* Translated by Barbara Haveland. New York: Farrar, Straus, Giroux, 1996.

Lewis, Richard S. Challenger: *The Final Voyage.* New York: Columbia University Press, 1988.

McConnell, Malcolm. Challenger: *A Major Malfunction.* New York: Doubleday, 1987.

Murray, Charles, and Catherine Bly Cox. *Apollo: The Race to the Moon.* New York and London: Simon and Schuster, 1989.

Oberg, James. "Dead Cosmonauts," *Uncovering Soviet Disasters.* New York: Random House, 1988.

Shayler, David. *Shuttle* Challenger: *Aviation Fact File.* Englewood Cliffs, N.J.: Prentice Hall, 1987.

Trento, Joseph. *Prescription for Disaster: From the Glory of Apollo to the Betrayal of the Shuttle.* New York: Crown, 1987.

Vaughan, Diane. *The* Challenger *Launch Decision: Risky Technology, Culture, and Deviance at NASA.* Chicago and London: University of Chicago Press, 1996.

WEBSITES

Challenger STS-51L Information
www.hq.nasa.gov/office/pao/History/sts51l

The Crew of the *Challenger* Shuttle Mission in 1986
www.hq.nasa.gov/office/pao/History/Biographies/challenger.html

"Modifications Completed to Space Shuttle Launch Pad 39-A,"
   Kennedy Space Center press release No. 125-89 (search on website)
spacelink.nasa.gov/index.html

Moonport, chapter 18, "The Fire That Seared the Spaceport"
www.hq.nasa.gov/office/pao/History/SP-4204/ch18-1

NASA Apollo Mission Summary–Apollo 1
www.hq.nasa.gov/office/pao/History/Apollo204

NASA Apollo 1–Kennedy Space Center
www.ksc.nasa.gov/history/apollo/apollo-1

Report of the Presidential Commission on the Space Shuttle Challenger *Accident*
www.ksc.nasa.gov/shuttle/missions/51-l/docs/rogers-commission/table-of-contents.html)

Shuttle Orbiter *Challenger,* Kennedy Space Center
www.ksc.nasa.gov/shuttle/resources/orbiters/challenger

Space Shuttle Annotated Bibliography
www.hq.nasa.gov/office/pao/History/Shuttlebib

Space Transportation Directorate: Advanced Space Transportation Program
stp.msfc.nasa.gov/

Further Reading

BOOKS

Billings, Charlene. *Christa McAuliffe.* Hillside, N.J.: Enslow Press, 1986.

Bond, Peter. *Heroes in Space: From Gagarin to Challenger.* Oxford, England: B. Blackwell, 1987.

Bredeson, Carmen. *Gus Grissom.* Hillside, N.J.: Enslow Press, 1998.

Cole, Michael. *Challenger.* Hillside, N.J.: Enslow Press, 1995.

Hohler, Robert T. *I Touch the Future: The Story of Christa McAuliffe.* New York: Random House, 1987.

Kennedy, Gregory. *The First Men in Space.* New York: Chelsea House, 1991.

Kennedy, Gregory. *Apollo to the Moon.* New York: Chelsea House, 1992.

Naden, Corinne J. and Rose Blue. *Christa McAuliffe.* Brookfield, Conn.: Millbrook Press, 1991.

Naden, Corinne J. *Ronald McNair.* Philadelphia: Chelsea House, 1991.

Schraff, Anne. *American Heroes of Exploration and Flight.* Hillside, N.J.: Enslow Press, 1996.

Westman, Paul. *John Young.* Minneapolis, Minn.: Dillon Press, 1981.

Wood, Leigh Hope. *Exploring Space.* Chicago, Ill.: Kids Books, Inc., 1996.

WEBSITES

Johnson Space Center
www.jsc.nasa.gov

Kennedy Space Center
www.ksc.nasa.gov

Mark Wade's Encyclopedia Astronautica
solar.rtd.utk.edu/~mwade/spaceflt.htm

The McAuliffe/*Challenger* Center
www.christa.org

The Men and Women of Space Team Online
quest.arc.nasa.gov/space/team/index.html

NASA
www.nasa.gov

National Aviation Hall of Fame
www.nationalaviation.org

National Women's Hall of Fame
www.greatwomen.org

Index

Index

and quality control, 42,
61, 85
National Research Council
(NRC), 107
Nelson, William, 78, 82
"New Nine," the, 23, 28
Nixon, Richard M., 52-53,
54
North American Aviation,
13, 40, 41, 42-43, 46, 48,
51
North American Rockwell,
54, 58

Onizuka, Ellison S., 76, 77
Orbiters, 54, 55, 56, 60,
63-66, 69, 90, 95, 109
"Original Seven," the , 21,
22, 27
O-rings, 59-60, 66-67, 86-
90, 102

Patsayev, Viktor, 35
Phillips, Samuel, 43, 107
"Phillips Report," 43
Presidential Commission,
99-103, 107
Project Vanguard, 18

Reagan, Ronald, 74, 78, 79,
95-96, 99
Resnik, Judith A., 76-77
Ride, Sally, 99, 105
Rocketdyne, 58
Rockwell International
Corporation, 58, 63, 90
Rogers, William, 99, 103

Safety improvements
after Apollo fire, 42,

46-47, 48
after *Challenger* accident,
102-106, 107, 108, 109
Salyut space station, 35, 53
Saturn rockets, 25
I-B rockets, 11, 27, 32
V rockets, 27
Schirra, Walter M., Jr., 21
Schweickart, Russell, 23
Scobee, Francis R. "Dick,"
74-75, 77, 93, 94, 98, 99
Scott, David, 23, 30
See, Elliott, 23
Senate, U.S., 42
Service module (SM), 25,
30, 42, 45
Shea, Joe, 32-36, 44, 47, 104
Shepard, Alan B., Jr., 21
Shuttle Avionics Integra-
tion Laboratory, 73
Shuttle Program Office,
103-4
Simpkinson, Scott, 41
Slayton, Donald "Deke,"
21, 32, 36, 37
Smith, Michael J., 75, 76,
93, 94, 98, 99, 104
Solid rocket boosters
(SRBs), 54, 56-57, 58,
59, 66, 87, 89, 91, 95,
96, 98, 102, 103, 104
Soviet Union, 17-18, 19,
34-35, 52
Soyuz 1, 34
Soyuz 2, 34
Soyuz 11, 34-35
"Space Mirror," 109
Space shuttle program,
53-109
Space Task Group, 53

Space Transportation
System (STS), 56, 58,
65, 68
Space walks, 22-23, 24, 28
Spartan-Halley satellite,
75, 83
Sputnik I, 17, 18
Sputnik II, 17
Stafford, Thomas, 23

Teacher in Space Project,
74, 78, 82, 88, 96
Thiokal, 58, 59-60, 66
Thompson, Floyd, 41
Tiles, heat-resistant, 57-58,
60, 63, 65, 66, 90-91
Tracking Data Relay
Satellite (TDRS), 83
Truly, Richard, 63, 103-4

Vanguard 1A rockets, 18
Vietnam War, 52, 74, 75
Volkov, Vladislav, 34-35
von Braun, Wernher, 19, 44
Vostok I, 21

Wear, Larry, 89
Webb, James, 40
White, Edward, II, 12-14,
23, 24, 28, 30-37, 45, 49
White Room, 32
Williams, C. C., 23

X-15 rocket plane, 42
X-24B, 74

Yeager, Chuck, 99
Young, John, 23, 24, 28,
66, 102, 105

Picture Credits

All photos courtesy of the National Aeronautics and Space Administration (NASA), except the following photographs:

page
18, 87: © Bettmann/Corbis   35: © Corbis   108: © Gina De Angelis

Cover Photos: All photos courtesy of the National Aeronautics and Space Administration (NASA)

GINA DE ANGELIS is a freelance author writer living in southern Virginia. She holds a B.A. from Marlboro College and an M.A. from the University of Mississippi. She is the author of more than a dozen Chelsea House books, including *The Black Cowboys, Morgan Freeman,* and *The Hindenburg.*

JILL McCAFFREY has served for four years as national chairman of the Armed Forces Emergency Services of the American Red Cross. Ms. McCaffrey also serves on the board of directors for Knollwood—the Army Distaff Hall. The former Jill Ann Faulkner, a Massachusetts native, is the wife of Barry R. McCaffrey, a member of President Bill Clinton's cabinet and director of the White House Office of National Drug Control Policy. The McCaffreys are the parents of three grown children: Sean, a major in the U.S. Army; Tara, an intensive care nurse and captain in the National Guard; and Amy, a seventh grade teacher. The McCaffreys also have two grandchildren, Michael and Jack.